JAPAN, 1941

REACTING TO THE PAST is an award-winning series of immersive role-playing games that actively engage students in their own learning. Students assume the roles of historical characters and practice critical thinking, primary source analysis, and argument, both written and spoken. Reacting games are flexible enough to be used across the curriculum, from first-year general education classes and discussion sections of lecture classes to capstone experiences, intersession courses, and honors programs.

Reacting to the Past was originally developed under the auspices of Barnard College and is sustained by the Reacting Consortium of colleges and universities. The Consortium hosts a regular series of conferences and events to support faculty and administrators.

Note to instructors: Before beginning the game you must download the Gamemaster's Materials, including an instructor's guide containing a detailed schedule of class sessions, role sheets for students, and handouts.

To download this essential resource, visit https://reactingconsortium.org/games, click on the page for this title, then click "Instructors Guide."

JAPAN, 1941

Between Pan-Asianism and the West

John E. Moser

REACTING
TO THE PAST

BARNARD

The University of North Carolina Press

Chapel Hill

Cover illustration: *Emperor Shōwa Army*, January 8, 1938. Photographer unknown, Wikimedia Commons.

ISBN 978-1-4696-7065-2 (pbk.: alk. paper)
ISBN 978-1-4696-7233-5 (e-book)

ABOUT THE AUTHOR

JOHN E. MOSER is professor of history at Ashland University, where he teaches courses on modern European, American, and East Asian history and serves as chair of Ashland's MA program in American History and Government. He is the author of four books, the most recent of which is *The Global Great Depression and the Coming of World War II*, which was published by Routledge in 2014. In 2016 John was the recipient of the Edward and Louaine Taylor Excellence in Teaching Award. In addition to *Japan, 1941: Between Pan-Asianism and the West* (W. W. Norton & Company) he is also the author of *Europe on the Brink, 1914: The July Crisis* and *Restoring the World, 1945: Security and Empire at Yalta* (both available through Reacting Consortium Press).

CONTENTS

JAPAN, 1941

PART 1: **INTRODUCTION**

BRIEF OVERVIEW OF THE GAME

It is September 1940. It has been just over three years since the beginning of the China Incident, in which Japan has sought by force to bring about an anti-Western, anti-Soviet partnership with China. Yet after a series of stunning victories, the war has settled into a frustrating stalemate. Worse, while officially neutral, the United States, Great Britain, and the Soviet Union have been assisting the Chinese and are threatening economic sanctions against Tokyo. With few natural resources of its own, Japan's industrial economy depends on imported raw materials—particularly oil.

However, Germany's recent conquests in Europe may have just presented Japan with a golden opportunity, as French, Dutch, and British possessions in Asia lay largely undefended. Taking on the roles of leading figures in Tokyo—army or navy officers, members of the Imperial Court, and others—you and your fellow players are thrust into the middle of Japan's strategic dilemma. Drawing on important works from Japan's past—addressing such topics as Bushido, the nature of the national entity (*kokutai*), and Pan-Asianism—you must advise the emperor on how to proceed. Will you call for a "strike south" to seize the natural resources of Southeast Asia—even at the risk of war with Britain and America? Or will you seek an understanding with those countries—even if it means giving up the ideal of a pan-Asian partnership? Similarly momentous decisions must also be made on domestic policy. How will Japan's increasingly scarce resources be allocated? Will the economy be subject to further state control?

PROLOGUE: "SPIRITUAL MOBILIZATION"

The Imperial Palace," the bus driver calls out.

The passengers and driver rise to their feet and bow reverently in the direction of the imposing stone walls of the Kikyomon Gate. You eagerly join them; like all good Japanese you believe that the emperor who resides behind that gate is a god, a direct descendant of the sun goddess, Amaterasu. Or at least you pretend to do so. You remember a time, not so long ago, when educated people such as yourself would privately scoff at the notion, but no more. Japan today can be a dangerous place for cynics. Reverence for the emperor is more than a patriotic duty—it is a religious obligation.

After a few seconds you and the others take your seats again and the bus resumes its course, belching a thick cloud of black smoke as it does so. Charcoal-burning vehicles have become the norm on the streets of Tokyo, having first made their appearance in 1938 in response to strict rationing of gasoline. You understand the need to conserve oil products—after all, Japan produces no petroleum, so it must rely wholly on foreign imports, particularly from the Dutch East Indies and the United States. You appreciate that it is in the national interest to keep such imports to a minimum, and of course the war effort in China has first claim on gasoline. Hence the charcoal-burning bus—although in two years you still haven't managed to get used to the smoke.

Gas isn't the only thing in short supply these days; it seems as though almost everything has been rationed. Matches and sugar were added to the list just last month. You recall that two years ago office workers and schoolchildren were encouraged to demonstrate a spirit of self-denial by eating "rising sun box lunches." These were nothing more than a single pickled plum on a bed of white rice. It was fitting that they did so, for "extravagance," we were told again and again, "is the enemy." These days even that meager fare seems extravagant, for white rice is becoming difficult to find.

The bus driver's voice interrupts your thoughts. "Ginza," he intones. You have reached your destination, Tokyo's famous shopping and entertainment district. Your position in the government has kept you so busy that it has actually been several years since you have been here, but given the fine summer weather this evening you thought you'd sample the nightlife. You rise, pay your fare, and step off onto the sidewalk of Chuo-dori, the district's main street. The bus moves on, engulfing you in another blast of thick black smoke.

More than any other part of Tokyo, the Ginza represents Japan's longtime fascination with the West. Even during the Tokugawa period it had been known for its shops, but it took on its present shape in 1872, after a fire had devastated much of this part of town. Fires, of course, had been nothing new to a city whose buildings were often nothing more than wood and paper. Had this fire occurred earlier, the Ginza would no doubt have been rebuilt largely in the traditional manner. But because it occurred only four years after the Meiji Restoration—when the old regime of the shōgun was overthrown in favor of one centered on the emperor—a wholly new Ginza emerged. This was a time when virtually everyone looked to the West for guidance; a time when "civilization and progress" meant imitating Western culture. An Irish-born architect named Thomas Waters oversaw the rebuilding of the district, which he filled with two- and three-story brick buildings built in the Georgian style. Through the center of the neighborhood runs a shopping promenade, open only to pedestrians and lined with department stores, dance halls, bars, theaters, and cafés.

Indeed, the café itself was a symbol of Japan's infatuation with the West. There were nearly fifty of them in the Ginza; the first—Kafe Raion (Café Lion)—opened in 1911. It was a conscious imitation of similar establishments in the United States, a place where city dwellers could eat Western-style food, drink Western-style beverages, and talk about national and world affairs. Patrons sat in chairs rather than on tatami mats, and they weren't obligated to remove their shoes. Respectable middle-class women could be found there, often even without male escorts. Kafe Raion became famous for its thick, juicy steaks (only 50 sen) and its provocatively dressed waitresses who flirted shamelessly with guests. You remember hearing rumors that at least some of them provided sexual services on the side.

Back in the 1920s the Ginza was the place to go, to shop, eat, drink, dance, or to see or be seen. On any given evening the streets were illuminated by neon lights, and filled with young men and women. *Moba* and *mogo*, they called themselves: a corruption of the English "modern boy" and "modern girl." The men wore bell-bottom trousers and spectacles inspired by the popular Hollywood actor Harold Lloyd, while the women created a sensation by going out in short skirts and bobbed—or, even more shocking, permed—hair.

In fact, English words had been heard and seen everywhere in those days, finding their way into the Japanese language particularly when it came to Western-style clothing. Everyone knew that pants had *poketto* (pockets), and that women wore *sukāto* (skirts) and *burajā* (bras), or on sunny days carried *parasōru* (parasols). Signs for cafés and restaurants commonly used Roman letters instead of Japanese characters, and even cigarettes had English names such as Cherry and Golden Bat. Cigarette-smoking, after all, was one of the more common Western practices adopted by the Japanese in the late nineteenth century.

It doesn't take you long to realize that the Ginza today is a very different place. No doubt the war in China—what the government calls the "China Incident"—has had something to do with it. The generals had originally promised that it would take no more than three months to resolve it, but that was nearly three years ago. Facing the reality of a long war, the first in the history of modern Japan, the government announced the "spiritual mobilization" of the entire country. The people had to be psychologically prepared for the ongoing struggle. Hundreds of thousands of young men are today fighting on the Asian continent; surely it cannot be too much to ask that civilians sacrifice as well.

This is all well and good, as far as you are concerned. Japan is fighting for the ideal of "Pan-Asianism"—that the countries of East Asia should unite against the threats of Western imperialism and Soviet Communism. China has been chronically unstable for generations, and the country's weakness has left it open to exploitation by outsiders—first the British; then the French, Russians, and Germans; and now the Soviets. Also, anyone with eyes and a brain can see that Communism has been a rising force in China; indeed, the leader of the Chinese Kuomintang (Nationalists), Jiang Jieshi, has been openly collaborating with the communists. If the communists should triumph, all of China would become a satellite of Soviet Russia. How could Japan be expected to protect itself from not one, but two gigantic communist countries so close to its borders?

Some claim that Japan seeks to conquer China, but nothing could be farther from the truth. Like many, you have heard dark rumors that the army has been colluding with organized crime—the infamous Yakuza—to sell opium to the Chinese in the hope of making them more docile. However, you regard these as seditious lies. All that Tokyo seeks is a pan-Asian partnership to defend East Asia from the European imperialists and the Soviet communists. However, the corrupt Jiang Jieshi would rather collaborate with Asia's enemies than make common cause with Japan. So be it. Until Jiang sees the error of his ways—or is overthrown—Japan must continue to fight, as the independence of all Asia is at stake.

Your attention moves back to the Ginza. The first thing you notice about it is that, although night is rapidly approaching, the once familiar neon lights are turned off—perhaps neon is now regarded as a pointless extravagance? As you step onto the promenade you see far fewer people than you remember. For a moment you wonder if this is the first of the month, which has been designated Public Service Day for Asia, in which all the shops, cafés, bars, and theaters are shut down by law. But no, that was three weeks ago—you remember because on that day your sister participated in a procession from the Yasukuni Shrine (the country's most sacred of sites, dedicated to the spirits of those soldiers who have died for the country) to the Imperial Palace. Still, there is little sign of the crowds that would have flocked to the Ginza ten years ago. Even the district's famous prostitutes are missing; recruited to service the troops in China, you've been told.

What's more, the people you do see out walking certainly don't look like *mobo* and *moga*. Most of the men are wearing the ill-fitting khaki civilian uniforms that were introduced last year. The women seem to be wearing *monpe* (simple pants) and blouses more commonly worn by peasants in the countryside. The women no longer wear makeup—that was banned last year—and they no longer have permanents, either: hairdressers have been instructed that no customer is to be given more than three curls. You also spot a sign as you walk along the promenade—"People with Permanents Will Please Refrain from Passing through Here."

Signs and posters certainly aren't in short supply. They're everywhere you look, in fact. "Extravagance Is the Enemy," says one, "Loyalty and Patriotism" another. The farther you walk, the more you see. "Respect Imperial Rescripts," "Untiring Perseverance," "Protect the Imperial Country," "Work for the Sake of the Country." Many are accompanied by images of soldiers, standing vigilant against some unseen enemy or being adored by trusting Chinese children.

You approach the Matsuzakaya, Japan's oldest department store (established in 1611) and decide to see what's inside. There's not much left on the shelves, and the few customers are rummaging through the little that's there. Signs everywhere advertise deep discounts on the remaining items, and the reason for the sale isn't hard to find. A couple of months ago the government announced that a prohibition of the sale of all nonessential goods will go into effect early in October, and stores have been doing all they can to sell off their inventories before then. "Extravagance is the enemy," after all.

As you browse you see several families with small children headed for the elevator. The children are excited about something, so you decide to follow. You find that they're going to the rooftop, which houses a swimming pool. Are they going for a swim? You realize as soon as the elevator doors open that this is not the case. A small crowd is gathered around the edges of the pool, blocking your view of the water, but you hear loud buzzing sounds coming from within. You come closer, and hear a voice booming from a loudspeaker. "See how the ships of the mighty Imperial Navy defeat our enemies!" You finally catch a glimpse of what is going on—a mock naval battle between electric boats. One bears the standard of the Imperial Japanese Navy; the other, the flag of the United States. That the country is not at war with the United States—not yet, at least—seems not to matter in the slightest to the spectators, who laugh and cheer as a wisp of smoke begins to rise from the U.S. boat.

In fact, you find yourself smiling at the scene, too. The Americans deserve this sort of abuse, and much worse. For the past forty years, every time Japan has tried to assert itself on the world stage, it's been the Americans who've tried to get in the way. They raise tariffs against our goods, pass laws that keep our people from settling in their country, issue protests when we try to protect our rights in China. They have a huge sphere of influence in Latin America, but when Japan tries to carve out something similar in Asia the Americans complain that we're interfering with something they call the "Open Door." *Open Door*—that's their code word for U.S. economic domination of Asia. The European empires are doomed, they know, but rather than let the people of Asia control their own destiny they seek to swoop in and take the place of the Europeans. In fact, you are certain that if it weren't for the meddling Americans Jiang Jieshi would have settled his differences with Japan long ago, but because Washington continues to send aid and encouragement he continues his pointless war to keep China in thrall to the West. Nobody you know wants a war against the United States—even the hotheads in the army—but the Americans need to realize that Japan isn't some third-rate power that can be pushed around. If they want a fight, then a fight they'll have.

But now you're getting yourself worked up. You came out tonight to get away from politics, so you take the elevator back down to the ground floor, pass by the display cases of Matsuzakaya, and go back out onto the promenade.

At the next corner you spot a newsstand, and decide to scan its contents. Here, too, you notice a big difference, for hundreds of newspapers and thousands of magazines have gone out of business in the past three years. Most of them were shut down by the government on the grounds that paper, like everything else, needed to be conserved for the war effort. Censorship has played a large role as well. In the 1920s, and even through the mid-1930s, Japan had a relatively free press. The only real restrictions came from the Peace Preservation Law of 1925, which made it a crime to advocate the abolition of private property or an overthrow of the existing order. Starting in 1937, though, a new press law has been enacted each year further limiting what can appear in print. Most editors today find it prudent to submit stories to the Home Ministry for approval rather than run the risk of being fined or imprisoned for publishing something that might be deemed harmful to the national interest. As a result, those newspapers that are still in print all look the same: the morning editions are limited to six pages, evening editions to four, all carrying the same stories that originate from the country's only wire service, Dōmei, which is owned by the government.

As you look over the newspapers and magazines, you are reminded that English-sounding words have virtually disappeared, as have Roman letters. Now all Japanese are supposed to call a pocket a *monoire* (put-things-in), a brassiere a *chichiosae* (breast restraint), the parasol a *yōhigara* (Western-style sun umbrella). Shop and café signs that only a few years ago sported Roman letters have been taken down, replaced by ones with traditional Japanese characters.

You come to a café and decide to stop in for a drink. You take a seat in the back corner, and after getting a waitress's attention you order a cup of sake. While you wait you listen to the radio broadcast that's being piped throughout the restaurant. Not long ago the sound of jazz would have come from every establishment in the Ginza; the biggest hits on the radio were Japanese covers of popular American songs, such as "Sing Me a Song of Araby" and "My Blue Heaven." One doesn't hear much jazz these days. The preferred form of music today is the march, such as "Patriotic March Song," 1.5 million copies of which have been sold in the two years since its release. There is "The Imperial Army Marches Off," "The Bivouac Song," "March of the Warships," and countless others. Even ballet has been co-opted by the military spirit: you remember reading a few days ago about a recent production called "Decisive Aerial Warfare Suite." Of course, a lot of this has to do with the fact that in 1934 the government acquired all of the radio stations in the country, organizing them into a massive public broadcasting corporation called NHK.

The waitress brings your sake, and you take a sip and grimace. Thanks to recent shortages of rice, sake has been made from sweet potatoes, and sometimes even from acorns. From the foul taste in your mouth you guess that this particular brew is acorn.

The music is interrupted by the evening war news report. There isn't much to it, of course—only a ten-minute announcement of some glorious victory in some far-away Chinese town of which you've never heard. There's a remarkable sameness to all of these news bulletins. Every engagement is a victory, of course, but there are also constant reminders of the selfless heroism of the troops. Each incident, no matter how minor, must feature a group of soldiers who go to their deaths rather than retreat or, worse yet, surrender to the enemy. The announcer keeps mentioning *Bushido*—the way of the warrior, made famous by the samurai of old. Just as those noble knights would freely sacrifice all in the service of their lords, our men in China are choosing death before dishonor in their service to the Emperor.

While you have no doubts about the valor of the Japanese Army, or the need to serve the Emperor, you wonder about this recent emphasis on Bushido. As a boy you remember a neighbor who fought in the Russo-Japanese War of 1904–05. He had been taken prisoner by the Russians, but you don't remember there being any particular shame associated with it. After he returned he was honored as a veteran just as anyone else. Today you would think that there was no greater dishonor than to be captured by the enemy; stories abound of men rushing headlong into enemy machine-gun fire, or blowing themselves up with hand grenades, rather than endure such a fate. One favorite is the story of the "Three Human Bombs," soldiers who were said to have strapped dynamite to their bodies and charged into the Chinese defenses at Shanghai. You can't help but wonder whether it's an entirely healthy way for an army to function.

You catch yourself gently shaking your head as the news bulletin continues, but you stop abruptly when you spot someone studying you carefully from a nearby table. You remember that since 1936 all cafés and dance halls have been under police surveillance; indeed, there have been increasing calls to close them altogether as places of frivolity, or even of pro-Western subversion. True, the man looking at you isn't wearing a police uniform, but these days that means little. He could easily be a member of the *Tokkō*—the "special higher police"—with the power to arrest anyone deemed subversive to public order, even without a warrant. Or he might be a member of some fanatical ultranationalist organization, the type that routinely assassinated politicians in the 1930s and even tried overthrowing the government four years ago. In the present environment even the mildest gesture, even from a figure of some importance such as yourself, might be interpreted as a sign of disloyalty.

To your immense relief the man looks away. Suddenly your plan for a carefree summer evening in the Ginza seems like a bad idea. You push aside your barely touched cup of acorn "sake," pay the waitress and head back outside to catch the next bus back home. It's still early, but that's just as well, for you are expected at a cabinet meeting next morning. German forces have recently conquered France and the Low Countries, and the fate of the European colonies in Southeast Asia suddenly seems very much in question. Some are calling this a golden opportunity for Japan to settle the China Incident and establish a new order for East Asia; others worry that any effort by Tokyo to take advantage of the situation will only inflame the Americans. But such talk can wait for the morning; at the moment all you can think of is your bed, and the promise of a good night's rest.

BASIC FEATURES OF REACTING TO THE PAST

Reacting to the Past is a series of historical role-playing games. Students are given elaborate game books that place them in moments of historical controversy and intellectual ferment. The class becomes a public body of some sort; students, in role, become particular individuals from the period, often as members of a faction. Their purpose is to advance a policy agenda and achieve their victory objectives. To do so, they will undertake research and write speeches and position papers, and they will also give formal speeches, participate in informal debates and negotiations, and otherwise work to win the game. After a few preparatory lectures, the game begins and the players are in charge; the instructor serves as adviser or "Gamemaster." Outcomes sometimes differ from the actual history; a postmortem session at the end of the game sets the record straight.

The following is an outline of what you will encounter in Reacting and what you will be expected to do. While these elements are typical of every Reacting game, it is important to remember that each game has its own special quirks.

1. Game Setup

Your instructor will spend some time before the beginning of the game helping you understand the historical background. During the setup period, you will read several different kinds of materials:

- The game book (which you are reading now), which includes historical information, rules and elements of the game, and essential documents.

- Your role sheet, which includes a short biography of the historical person you will model in the game as well as that person's ideology, objectives, responsibilities, and resources. Your role may be an actual figure or a composite.

In addition to the game book, you may also be required to read primary and secondary sources (perhaps including one or more accompanying books), which provide further information and arguments for use during the game. Often you will be expected to conduct research to bolster your papers and speeches.

Read all of this contextual material and all of these documents and sources before the game begins. And just as important, go back and reread these materials throughout the game. A second reading while *in role* will deepen your understanding and alter your perspective because ideas take on a different aspect when seen through the eyes of a partisan actor.

Players who have carefully read the materials and who know the rules of the game will invariably do better than those who rely on general impressions and uncertain recollections.

2. Game Play

Once the game begins, certain players preside over the class sessions. These presiding officers may be elected or appointed. Your instructor then becomes the Gamemaster (GM) and takes a seat in the back of the room. While not in control, the GM may do any of the following:

- Pass notes to spur players to action

- Announce the effects of actions taken during the game on outside parties (e.g., neighboring countries) or the effects of outside events on game actions (e.g., a declaration of war)

- Interrupt and redirect proceedings that have gone off track

Presiding officers may act in a partisan fashion, speaking in support of particular interests, but they must observe basic standards of fairness. As a fail-safe device, most Reacting games employ the "Podium Rule," which allows a player who has not been recognized to approach the podium and wait for a chance to speak. Once at the podium, the player has the floor and must be heard.

In order to achieve your objectives, outlined in your role sheet, you must persuade others to support you. You must speak with others, because never will a role sheet contain all that you need to know and never will one faction have the strength to prevail without allies. Collaboration and coalition building are at the heart of every game.

Most role sheets contain secret information that you are expected to guard. Exercise caution when discussing your role with others. You may be a member of a faction, which gives you allies who are generally safe and reliable, but even they may not always be in total agreement with you.

In games where factions are tight-knit groups with fixed objectives, finding a persuadable ally can be difficult. Fortunately, every game includes roles that are undecided (or "Indeterminate") about certain issues. Everyone is predisposed on certain issues, but most players can be persuaded to support particular positions. Cultivating these players is in your interest. (By contrast, if you are assigned an Indeterminate role, you will likely have considerable freedom to choose one or another side in the game; but often, too, Indeterminates have special interests of their own.)

Cultivate friends and supporters. Before you speak at the podium, arrange to have at least one supporter second your proposal, come to your defense, or admonish those in the body not paying attention. Feel free to ask the presiding officer to assist you, but appeal to the GM only as a last resort.

Immerse yourself in the game. Regard it as a way to escape imaginatively from your usual self—and your customary perspective as a college student in the twenty-first century. At first, this may cause discomfort because you may be advocating ideas that are incompatible with your own beliefs. You may also need to take actions that you would find reprehensible in real life. Remember that a Reacting game is only a game and that you and the other players are merely playing roles. When other players offer criticisms, they are not criticizing you as a person. Similarly, you must never criticize another person in the game. But you will likely be obliged to criticize their persona. (For example, never say, "Sally's argument is ridiculous." But feel free to say, "Governor Winthrop's argument is ridiculous." though you would do well to explain exactly why!) Always assume, when spoken to by a fellow player—whether in class or out of class—that that person is speaking to you in role.

Help create this world by avoiding the colloquialisms and familiarities of today's college life. Never should the presiding officer, for example, open a session with the salutation, "Hi guys." Similarly, remember that it is inappropriate to trade on out-of-class relationships when asking for support within the game. ("Hey, you can't vote against me. We're both on the tennis team!")

Reacting to the Past seeks to approximate of the complexity of the past. Because some people in history were not who they seemed to be, so, too, some roles in Reacting may include elements of conspiracy or deceit. (For example, Brutus did not announce to the Roman Senate his plans to assassinate Caesar.) If you are assigned such a role, you must make it clear to everyone that you are merely playing a role. If, however, you find yourself in a situation where you find your role and actions to be stressful or uncomfortable, tell the GM.

3. Game Requirements

Your instructor will explain the specific requirements for your class. In general, however, a Reacting game will require you to perform several distinct but interrelated activities:

Reading

This standard academic work is carried on more purposefully in a Reacting course, since what you read is put to immediate use.

Research and Writing

The exact writing requirements depend on your instructor, but in most cases you will be writing to persuade others. Most of your writing will take the form of policy statements, but you might also write autobiographies, clandestine messages, newspaper articles, or aftergame reflections. In most cases papers are posted on the class website for examination by others. Basic rules: Do not use big fonts or large margins. Do not simply repeat your position as outlined in your role sheet: You must base your arguments on historical facts as well as ideas drawn from the assigned texts *and* from independent research. (Your instructor will outline the requirements for footnoting and attribution.) Be sure to consider the weaknesses in your argument and address them; if you do not your opponents will.

Public Speaking and Debate

Most players are expected to deliver at least one formal speech from the podium (the length of the game and the size of the class will affect the number of speeches). Reading papers aloud is seldom effective. Some instructors may insist that students instead speak freely from notes. After a speech, a lively and even raucous debate will likely ensue. Often the debates will culminate in a vote.

Strategizing

Communication among students is a pervasive feature of Reacting games. You should find yourself writing emails, texting, and attending meetings on a fairly regular basis. If you do not, you are being outmaneuvered by your opponents.

4. Skill Development

A recent Associated Press article on education and employment made the following observations:

> The world's top employers are pickier than ever. And they want to see more than high marks and the right degree. They want graduates with so-called soft skills—those who can work well in teams, write and speak with clarity, adapt quickly to changes in technology and business conditions, and interact with colleagues from different countries and cultures. [. . .] And companies are going to ever-greater lengths to identify the students who have the right mix of skills, by observing them in role-playing exercises to see how they handle pressure and get along with others [. . .] and [by] organizing contests that reveal how students solve problems and handle deadline pressure.

Reacting to the Past, probably better than most elements of the curriculum, provides the opportunity for developing these soft skills. This is because you will be practicing persuasive writing, public speaking, critical thinking, problem solving, and collaboration. You will also need to adapt to changing circumstances and work under pressure.

PART 2: **HISTORICAL BACKGROUND**

East Asia and the Pacific Region, 1940

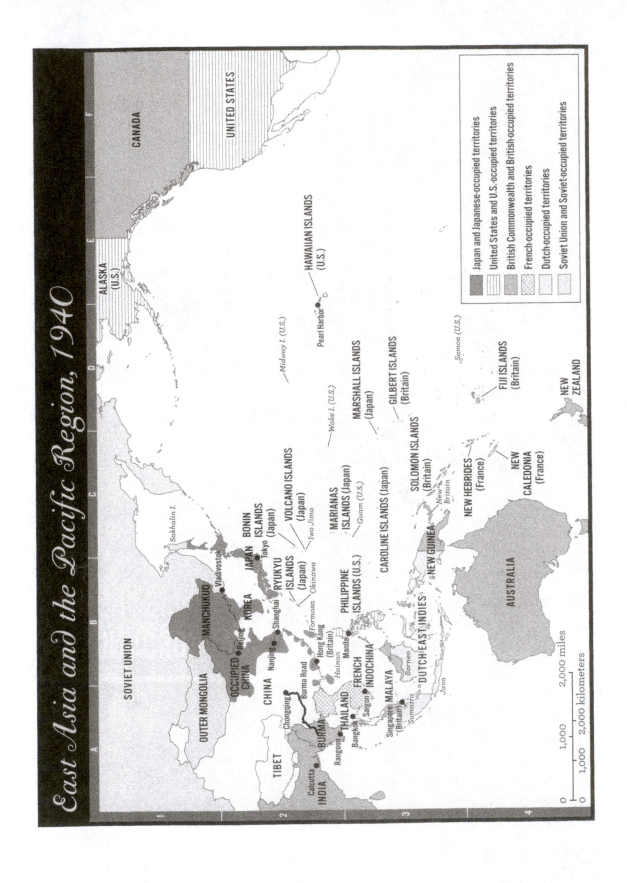

Legend:
- Japan and Japanese-occupied territories
- United States and U.S.-occupied territories
- British Commonwealth and British-occupied territories
- French-occupied territories
- Dutch-occupied territories
- Soviet Union and Soviet-occupied territories

SOVIET UNION
CANADA
UNITED STATES
ALASKA (U.S.)
HAWAIIAN ISLANDS (U.S.)
Pearl Harbor
Midway I. (U.S.)
Wake I. (U.S.)
MARSHALL ISLANDS (Japan)
GILBERT ISLANDS (Britain)
Samoa (U.S.)
FIJI ISLANDS (Britain)
NEW CALEDONIA (France)
NEW ZEALAND
NEW HEBRIDES (France)
SOLOMON ISLANDS (Britain)
New Britain
NEW GUINEA
CAROLINE ISLANDS (Japan)
MARIANAS ISLANDS (Japan)
Guam (U.S.)
VOLCANO ISLANDS (Japan)
Iwo Jima
BONIN ISLANDS (Japan)
JAPAN
Tokyo
RYUKYU ISLANDS (Japan)
Okinawa
Formosa
Sakhalin I.
Vladivostok
MANCHUKUO
KOREA
Shanghai
Beijing
Nanjing
OCCUPIED CHINA
OUTER MONGOLIA
TIBET
CHINA
Chongqing
Burma Road
INDIA
Calcutta
BURMA
Rangoon
THAILAND
Bangkok
FRENCH INDOCHINA
Saigon
Hainan
Hong Kong (Britain)
Manila
PHILIPPINE ISLANDS (U.S.)
MALAYA
Singapore (Britain)
Sumatra
Borneo
Java
DUTCH EAST INDIES
AUSTRALIA

0   1,000   2,000 miles
0   1,000   2,000 kilometers

A   B   C   D   E   F
1
2
3
4

CHRONOLOGY, 1914–40

August 1914   **Outbreak of World War I**   Japan declares war on Germany under the terms of the Anglo-Japanese Alliance, seizing the German-held Shandong Peninsula as well as German colonies in the Pacific.

January 1915   **Presentation of Twenty-One Demands to China**   Japan demands Chinese recognition of Japanese control of the Shandong Peninsula as well as extensive concessions elsewhere in China. Lacking support from abroad, China grudgingly accepts most terms.

May 1919   **Anti-Japanese Protests in China**   Protestors denounce the intention of the Allies to award the Shandong Peninsula to Japan in the Versailles Treaty and impose a boycott of Japanese goods.

June 1919   **Signing of the Treaty of Versailles**   The treaty formally concludes the war against Germany and awards Japan a number of former German colonies in East Asia and the Pacific, including the Shandong Peninsula. Japan also asks that a clause be included affirming the equality of the races, but Great Britain and the United States reject the proposal.

November 1921– February 1922   **Washington Conference**   The United States calls this conference to discuss naval arms limitation and East Asian affairs. Japan promises in the Nine Power Pact to respect China's territorial integrity and the principle of the Open Door. Japan also promises to restore the Shandong Peninsula to China and signs a treaty limiting size of Japanese navy to three-fifths that of the United States and Great Britain. The announcement of the treaty results in nationalist riots in Japan.

September 1923	**Kantō earthquake** The natural disaster kills some 150,000 people in the Tokyo–Yokohama region. Police kill a number of left-wing and labor activists whom they accuse of planning a revolution.
May 1924	**U.S. Immigration Act** The U.S. government's decision to impose a total exclusion of Japanese immigrants leads to widespread demonstrations and a boycott of American goods.
May 1925	**Enactment of Peace Preservation Law in Japan** The law makes it a crime to advocate any alteration in Japan's *kokutai* (national entity) or to call for the abolition of private property. By the end of the decade nearly 2,000 are arrested under this law.
December 1926	**Ascension of Hirohito to the Japanese throne** Upon the death of his father, Yoshihito—better known in Japan as the Taishō emperor—Hirohito becomes emperor of Japan. The name chosen for his reign is Shōwa, which translates as "enlightened peace."
August 1928	**Signing of the Kellogg–Briand Pact** Japan joins the United States, France, Germany, Belgium, Great Britain, Australia, New Zealand, South Africa, Ireland, Canada, Italy, Poland, and Czechoslovakia in signing an agreement renouncing war "as an instrument of national policy."
April 1930	**Signing of London Naval Treaty** Despite intense opposition by many naval officers, Tokyo agrees to extend limits to the fleet size first established in Washington in 1922.
November 1930	**Assassination attempt against Prime Minister Hamaguchi** The would-be assassin is a civilian member of a secret ultranationalist organization, outraged by Hamaguchi's efforts to reduce military spending. The prime minister is hospitalized for several months but returns to his post in March 1931.

March 1931 **Coup attempt in Tokyo** Young army officers belonging to a secret society called the *Sakurakai* (Cherry Blossom Society) attempt to foment riots that would give the army an excuse to topple the civilian government and establish a military dictatorship. The coup collapses when riots fail to materialize and key generals refuse to support the effort. The affair is hushed up, and the plotters receive only mild punishments.

September 1931 **Japanese occupation of Manchuria** During night maneuvers in Shenyang (Mukden), the Kwantung Army sets explosive charges on a stretch of railway line, then uses the resulting blast as an excuse to occupy all of Manchuria.

February 1932 **Republic of Manchukuo proclaimed** With the Japanese occupation of Manchuria near completion, the Kwantung Army proclaims the state of Manchukuo. This is widely seen as a puppet government controlled by the Japanese Army.

March 1932 **League of Blood Incident** Members of the ultranationalist group *Ketsumeidan* (League of Blood) set out to assassinate prominent businessmen and succeed in murdering Dan Takuma of the Mitsui Corporation as well as former Finance Minister Junnosuke Inoue. The assassins receive life sentences but are paroled in 1940.

May 1932 **Assassination of Prime Minister Inukai** Blaming Prime Minister Inukai for Japan's adherence to the London Naval Treaty, a group of eleven navy officers attempt a coup d'état by assassinating Inukai and launching simultaneous attacks against other allegedly pro-Western Japanese leaders. Although Inukai is killed, the coup comes to nothing, and the assassins are arrested and court-martialed. Ultimately all eleven receive very light sentences.

February 1933 **Japanese withdrawal from League of Nations** The league votes to brand Japan an aggressor for its actions in Manchuria. The Japanese delegation, headed by Matsuoka Yōsuke, storms out of the proceedings and announces its intent to leave the organization entirely. The league takes no further action against Japan.

May 1933	**Tanggu Truce in Manchuria** With the Japanese military occupation of all of Manchuria, the nationalist government accepts the Tanggu Truce, accepting a demilitarized zone in northeast China under Japanese control.
April 1934	**Amau Declaration** In light of the Japanese military successes in northeast China, the Japanese Foreign Office announces a virtual protectorate over China in its relations with the Western powers.
December 1934	**Japanese renunciation of the naval treaties** The Japanese government formally announces that it will no longer regard itself as bound by the terms of the Washington Naval Treaty of 1922 and the London Naval Treaty of 1930.
February 1936	**February 26 Incident** In an uprising of young army officers in Tokyo, the Japanese finance minister, Viscount Saito, and several other prominent figures are assassinated. The rebels seek to establish a military dictatorship in Japan and occupy central Tokyo for several days. The revolt is crushed on direct orders from the emperor, and in July a military court sentences seventeen of the rebels to death.
August 1936	**Fundamental Principles of National Policy** The cabinet of Hirota Koki announces that Japan's policy is to rid East Asia of Soviet influence as well as to expand into Southeast Asia and the South Pacific. In order to accomplish this, the document calls for an army large enough to take on that of the Soviet Union and a navy capable of defeating the United States.
November 1936	**Anti-Comintern Pact** The German and Japanese governments, joined later by the Italian government, sign an agreement to combat global Communism.

December 1936   **Kidnapping of Jiang Jieshi**   General Zhang Xueliang kidnaps Jiang Jieshi in an effort to force Jiang to declare war against the Japanese. Demonstrations of support for Jiang erupt across China, including among the communist Chinese. These demonstrations force Zhang to release Jiang, but the following month Jiang concludes an agreement with the communists to cooperate against the Japanese.

March 1937   **Publication of *Fundamentals of Our National Entity***   Written by a committee of academics and government officials, this book affirms the emperor's divinity. Further, it blames many of Japan's recent problems on the spread of Western ideas such as individualism and rationalism.

July 1937   **Marco Polo Bridge Incident; beginning of the Sino-Japanese War**   During night maneuvers, Japanese troops clash with Chinese forces outside Beijing. The fighting quickly spreads to other parts of China, reflecting Japanese preparations for a general war, although war is not formally declared. The Japanese navy announces a blockade of the Chinese coast, and Beijing, Tianjin, and Shanghai quickly fall to the invaders.

December 1937   ***Panay* Incident**   Japanese aircraft attack U.S. and British warships on the Yangtze River near Nanjing resulting in the loss of the American gunboat the U.S.S. *Panay*. The Franklin D. Roosevelt administration eventually accepts a Japanese apology and promise of compensation for the attack, but Japanese forces continue to violate foreign property and rights in China.

December 1937– January 1938   **Nanjing Massacre**   After heavy fighting, the Japanese occupy Nanjing, where over the next six weeks they commit horrible atrocities against Chinese civilians. There is a huge international outcry against Tokyo, and Jiang Jieshi promises that there will be no compromises with the Japanese that would result in any loss of Chinese territory or independence.

March 1938	**Enactment of National Mobilization Law in Japan** Pushed through the Diet by Prime Minister Konoye Fumimaro, the new law provides for government control over labor unions, nationalization of certain industries, and wage and price controls. It also ensures the army and navy virtually unlimited budgets. Although originally attacked as unconstitutional, it ultimately passes thanks to strong pressure from the army, navy, and bureaucracy.
July–August 1938	**Soviet–Japanese fighting in eastern Siberia** Japanese and Soviet forces clash at Changkufeng, near the border of Siberia, Korea, and Manchukuo. Although the two governments agree to a truce, tensions between Russia and Japan remained volatile.
May–September 1939	**Fighting between Soviet and Japanese forces at Nomonhan** Serious fighting breaks out along the Mongolian frontier between Japanese and Russian forces. After suffering heavy losses at the hands of the Red Army, the Japanese agree to a truce.
July 1939	**U.S. terminates the Trade Pact of 1911 with Japan** The Franklin D. Roosevelt administration announces its intention to withdraw from the Trade Pact of 1911 with Japan in protest against Tokyo's ongoing war against China. Trade between the two countries continues on a day-to-day basis, but the United States reserves the right to impose sanctions if Japanese aggression continues.
August 1939	**Soviet–German Non-Aggression Pact** The announcement that the German and Soviet governments had signed a non-aggression pact is regarded in Tokyo as a betrayal, considering that Germany and Japan had concluded the Anti-Comintern Pact only three years earlier.
September 1939	**World War II begins in Europe** German armed forces launch a concerted attack on Poland, causing Great Britain and France to declare war on Germany. Within four weeks Poland is conquered.

March 1940	**Pro-Japanese government established in China** The Japanese Army sets up a new Chinese government under Wang Jingwei in Nanjing as a counterweight to the Nationalist Chinese government and to administer the regions of China under Japanese control.
April–June 1940	**German offensives in the west** German forces launch a series of offensives that succeed in conquering Denmark, Norway, the Netherlands, Belgium, and France, all in the course of three months.
July 1940	**Closure of the Burma Road** Under intense pressure from the Japanese government, Great Britain promises to close the Burma Road, an important route for British and U.S. aid to Jiang Jieshi's China.
July 1940	**Fall of the Yonai cabinet** Japan's army minister, Hata Shunroku, increasingly frustrated by what he perceives as timidity on the part of prime minister, resigns from the cabinet. When the army fails to appoint a replacement, Yonai is forced to step down.

JAPAN BETWEEN ASIA AND THE WEST, 1853–1940

Commodore Perry and the End of Sakoku

The origins of Japan's dilemma in 1940 can be traced back to 1853, when four U.S. warships under the command of Commodore Matthew Perry steamed into Edo (today Tokyo) Bay. The men aboard those ships encountered a Japan that had changed very little for more than 200 years. The country's economy was agrarian: the vast majority of the population was engaged in the cultivation of rice. It was governed by an elite class known as the samurai—warriors, at least in theory, but because Japan had been at peace for so long, they were more administrators than soldiers. At the apex of Japan's political structure stood the shōgun, roughly translated as "commander in chief," a position that remained in the hands of the immensely powerful Tokugawa clan. There was also an emperor, but although he was believed to have descended from Amaterasu Ōmikami, the sun goddess, his position was merely ceremonial. The emperor remained ensconced in Kyoto—to this day recognized as the cultural capital of Japan—while the shōgun ruled from his palace in Edo, the country's largest city.

Since the early seventeenth century Japan had remained relatively isolated under the Tokugawa shōgun. Before that there had been considerable activity by merchants and missionaries from Portugal, Spain, the Netherlands, and England. However, the reigning Tokugawa shōgun, Tokugawa Iemitsu, feared that trade might ultimately be the opening wedge for foreign domination of the country. He was particularly concerned about the spread of Christianity in Japan, thanks to the work of Spanish and Portuguese missionaries. Therefore, in a series of edicts issued during the 1630s the shōgun initiated a policy of *sakoku* (closed country), in which Japanese were forbidden from leaving, and Westerners were prohibited from entering. Japan was never completely secluded, as trade continued with other East Asian nations, and even some limited trade with the West was allowed to continue through a group of specially licensed Dutch merchants in Nagasaki. For the most part, however, Japan spent the next two centuries shielded from Western ideas and influences.

Sakoku, "closed country," refers to the policy employed by the Tokugawa shōguns of promoting internal harmony by limiting the country's exposure to foreign ideas. Although it did not close off the country entirely, it did succeed for about 220 years in restricting ordinary people's access to Christianity and other potentially subversive ideas.

The arrival of Commodore Perry's steamships in 1853 dealt the death blow to sakoku. Perry demanded that Japan abandon its isolation and accept a trade treaty with the United States; the shōgun, Tokugawa Iesada, awed by the power of Western technology, felt he had little choice but to comply. Over the next several years other powers arrived, including Great Britain, France, and Russia; each made similar threats and demands. At the same time the country began once again to absorb Western ideas—particularly Western science and technology—and so successfully adapted them that by the end of the nineteenth century Japan was well on its way to becoming an industrial power itself. Still, for a country with a proud military tradition, dominated by the values of the samurai, subservience to the West was a bitter pill to swallow. The decision to submit to the demands of the Americans—as well as to similar demands by the British, French, and other Westerners who followed closely in Perry's wake—destabilized the shōgun's regime and would lead to the so-called Meiji Restoration of 1868. In that watershed event, the title of shōgun was abolished, and the emperor, who had for centuries served as no more than a figurehead, moved from Kyoto to the capital city, now renamed Tokyo, and was recognized as absolute ruler. The new governing structure also possessed a number of Western features, such as a written constitution, a governing cabinet appointed by the emperor, and an elected legislature.

The "Spirit of Civilization"

The men who brought about the Meiji Restoration had mixed attitudes toward the West. On one hand, their rallying cry had been *sonnō jōi* (revere the emperor, expel the barbarians) so they certainly harbored their share of resentment against foreigners. At the same time, however, they believed their country was suffering from its current humiliations as a result of its technological backwardness, and that if Japan were ever to free itself from foreign oppression it would have to learn from its enemies. Their goal, therefore, was to adopt Western military and industrial technologies without losing Japan's essential "spirit."

Some went further than this, however. In the early 1870s a group of intellectuals formed a group called the *Meirokusha*, the goal of which was "to promote civilization and enlightenment." The members of this organization claimed that Japan's humiliation was a wake-up call, and that the nation's weakness was the result of the "superstition, irrationality, ignorance, and backwardness of its people." The leading figure of the Meirokusha was Fukuzawa Yukichi, who in the 1860s had traveled to both the United States and Europe and served as chief translator for the shōgun's government. Fukuzawa insisted that simply learning Western technological methods was insufficient; a national renewal, he argued, would require a new mindset on the part of the Japanese. As he wrote in 1872:

> Schools, industries, armies and navies are the mere external forms of civilization. They are not difficult to produce. All that is needed is the money to pay for them. Yet there remains something immaterial, something that cannot be seen or heard, bought or sold, lent or borrowed. It pervades the whole nation and its influence is so strong that without it none of the schools or the other external forms would be of the slightest use. This supremely important thing we must call the spirit of civilization.[1]

This "spirit of civilization," which Fukuzawa believed the West possessed but Japan (as well as the other countries of East Asia) did not, encompassed the following:

- **The "spirit of independence,"** by which Fukuzawa meant the realization that all human beings are born free and equal in moral worth and possess importance as individuals. He complained that indoctrination with Confucian philosophy, which emphasized hierarchy, had left the common people of Japan "slavish and servile. [. . .] They are just as meek and obedient as pet dogs."[2] Such people might be taught certain methods, but would remain so uncritical of authority that they could never bring lasting reform for their country.

- **The "spirit of rationality,"** in which individuals rejected superstitions and behaved in a manner that reflected the use of reason, rather than unthinking reliance on tradition or the example of others. This, Fukuzawa argued, was the true wellspring of science—a sense of skepticism toward received knowledge and a willingness to seek answers for oneself. Paradoxically, he sometimes criticized along these lines those who enthusiastically embraced Western trends, claiming that they often did so for the wrong reasons. For example, he believed that it was eminently reasonable for a Japanese man to have his hair styled in Western fashion, but he feared that many of his countrymen were doing so simply because Western styles had become popular. Rather, Western hairstyles were good because they allowed the hair to serve its natural function of keeping one's head warm, as opposed to the traditional Japanese style of shaving the top of the head.

- The **"spirit of enterprise,"** in which it was acceptable for individuals to pursue their self-interest. This meant not being afraid to attempt to improve one's place in society, rather than passively accepting the station into which one was born. It meant that it was acceptable—even commendable—to seek one's own happiness according to one's own criteria, whether this meant by financial success or some other standard. At the same time, it meant accepting personal responsibility for one's condition.

- The **"spirit of progress,"** in which individuals recognized that civilization was not simply a means to wealth and military power, but rather a stage in a larger process by which humankind moved ever closer to perfection. Japan, he claimed, had passed through earlier stages such as *konton* (primitive chaos) and *yaban* (savagery), and now stood at *hankai* (semi-civilization). Although Europeans and Americans still had much more progress to make, they had reached *bummei* (civilization), and Japan must now seek to do likewise.

Due in part to efforts by Fukuzawa and the other Meirokusha intellectuals, Japan in the initial years after the restoration appeared to be deluged with the trappings of Western society, particularly in the cities. The eating of pork and beef, long prohibited by religious tradition, became a common practice. Western fashions grew popular, both in civilian and military life—the army and navy both adopted uniforms based on those of Western armed forces, and even the emperor himself donned a Western-style uniform. Urban skylines increasingly came to be dominated by skyscrapers built according to Western architectural designs.

The Reassertion of Tradition

The rapid spread of Western ideas could not help but provoke a reaction, and even at the time complaints could be heard that Westernization was going too far. Motoda Nagazane, an educational adviser to the Meiji emperor, denounced what he saw as efforts "to convert Japanese into facsimiles of Europeans and Americans" and specifically argued against the use of Western textbooks in Japanese public schools. The encouragement of individualism, he claimed, would turn students into troublemakers and delinquents. Instead young Japanese should be trained in "the Imperial ancestral precepts" of "benevolence, duty, loyalty, and filial piety."[3]

Part of the reaction against Western culture was a growing belief that, as the only East Asian country to rise to world power status while resisting European colonialism, Japan had an historic role to play as the champion of **Pan-Asianism**. Advocates of this view held that Japan represented a specifically Asian path toward modernity, one that could and should be followed by countries such as Korea and China. European imperialism stood in the way of this goal; therefore, Japan must do more than simply serve as a model—it must also strive to liberate East Asia from foreign domination.

> **Pan-Asianism** was the belief that the nations of Asia needed to join together to protect the continent from encroachments from the West. Japanese supporters of Pan-Asianism usually believed their nation, as the most technologically advanced of the Asian states, was destined to play a leading role in bringing about this union.

During the late nineteenth century such attitudes served merely as a check against what otherwise might have grown into a tendency to abandon all that was traditionally Japanese in favor of Western attitudes. However, anti-Western sentiment began to harden in the early twentieth century. It found its clearest expression in the proliferation of organizations calling for the return to traditional agrarian values, the elimination of capitalism (associated with Japan's massive corporations, the *zaibatsu*), the purging from Japanese culture of Western influences, and an aggressive foreign policy aimed at liberating East Asia from Western imperialism. Many of these called themselves **traditionalists**, and in some ways they did invoke the values of an earlier time in Japanese history, but to a large extent the tradition they championed was borrowed selectively and adapted to suit their purposes and, in some cases, wholly invented.

> The term *traditionalists* in any context refers to those who defend old ideas in the face of challenges from new ones. Japanese traditionalists tended to uphold the country's old warrior culture; the belief in the divinity of the emperor; and the communal values of the Japanese countryside against the threat of Western science, skepticism, and individualism.

This upsurge in traditionalism coincided with a more aggressive Japanese foreign policy—made possible, ironically, by the modern developments that traditionalists decried. As early as 1879 the new Japanese army, made up of conscript soldiers and commanded by former samurai, seized the Ryukyu Islands, but starting in the 1890s Tokyo set its eyes on larger prizes. In 1894 it provoked a war against a tottering Chinese Empire and, after defeating its army and navy, conquered both Korea and Taiwan. It then sought to expand its influence into the Chinese province of Manchuria, placing the country on a collision course with Russia. The result was the Russo-Japanese War of 1904–05, in which the Japanese armed forces shocked the world by defeating the Russians on land and sea. Although Manchuria remained formally part of China, Japanese influence, including control of the railroads, replaced that of Russia. In addition, the southern half of Sakhalin Island passed from Russia to Japan.

The United States and the "Open Door" in China

Japan's aggressive expansion in East Asia brought the country into conflict with the United States, as it became clear that the two were pursuing contradictory goals in the region. The United States had become an active player in East Asian affairs in 1898, when U.S. forces captured the Philippine Islands from the Spanish. Soon afterward the administration of William McKinley made it clear that the country had significant interests in that area. In the famous Open Door Note of 1900 U.S. Secretary of State John Hay asked that Japan and the great powers of Europe respect China's territorial integrity as well as the principle of equal access to Chinese markets. No power, Hay claimed, should possess any exclusive rights over any part of China. While there was little that the United States could do to enforce the **Open Door Policy**, it would remain the basis for U.S. policy in Asia for most of the twentieth century. It also laid the groundwork for conflict with Japan, which insisted that it deserved a special position in China thanks to the two countries' geographical proximity to one another. The Open Door struck Japanese leaders as hypocritical. Under the Monroe Doctrine the United States had claimed a special connection with the states of Latin America, warning European nations that their presence in the region was unwelcome. All that Tokyo wanted, government spokesmen asserted, was an "Asiatic Monroe Doctrine."

> The **Open Door Policy**, first enunciated by U.S. Secretary of State John Hay, called on the great powers to respect China's territorial integrity and to allow all countries' products to have equal access to Chinese markets. The Open Door would be the guiding principle behind U.S. foreign policy in East Asia for roughly the next fifty years.

Tensions between the United States and Japan began to simmer after 1911, when a revolution in China overthrew the emperor. A new republic was declared, but within a few years the central government in Beijing had lost control over most of the country, where local warlords operated as independent rulers. Sensing that the instability in China endangered Japanese interests there, Tokyo issued the Twenty-One Demands to Beijing in 1915. Among its terms was a significant expansion of Japan's **sphere of influence** in the country, and the reorganization of the Chinese police force under Japanese supervision. Tokyo threatened war if its demands were not met, leading China to appeal to the Western powers. The United States responded by reaffirming the principle of the Open Door, but a diplomatic crisis was averted in 1917 when the two countries signed the Lansing-Ishii Agreement. According to this document Japan promised to respect the Open Door, while the United States recognized that Japan had "special interests" in China. These terms contradicted one another, but as both countries were at the time fighting against Germany, the underlying disagreement was temporarily papered over.

> A **sphere of influence** is a region in a country in which some other country possesses special rights or privileges—for example, that country's goods might not be subject to tariffs or its citizens might be exempt from local laws. In the early twentieth century Japan and several European nations possessed spheres of influence in China.

Japan's Pro-Western Foreign Policy

One important reason Tokyo was willing to back away from some of its Twenty-One Demands was the Japanese government's decision in the 1910s and 1920s on a pro-British and pro-American policy. This orientation could be seen in a whole series of initiatives, including the following:

- Japan declared war on Germany in 1914, in return for which Tokyo received much of Germany's former empire in East Asia and the Pacific.

- Japan signed treaties in Washington, D.C. in 1922 and in London in 1930, under which it promised to respect the status quo in Asia and limit its navy to only three-fifths the size of those of Great Britain and the United States.

- Japan returned the Shandong peninsula (which its forces captured from Germany in 1914) to China in 1922.

In each instance, Japanese leaders were willing to act as they did because the country's economy was booming, based largely on its trade with the West. In the eyes of the leaders of Japan's largest political parties, as well as the **zaibatsu**, any policy that might offend the United States would be bad for business, and therefore bad for the country.

Japan's willingness to participate in a global order led by the United States and Great Britain began to wane not long after the end of World War I. As one of the victorious Allies, Japan sent a delegation to Paris to participate in peace negotiations. But while the diplomats succeeded in winning control of Germany's former Pacific colonies, their efforts to secure a clause in the final treaty asserting "the equality of nations" were thwarted by the British and Americans. To the Japanese, who believed that their industrial and military prowess entitled them to a position of respect in the world community, the Allies' rejection of the equality clause was a slap in the face. Their wounded pride would be inflamed even further in 1924, when the U.S. Congress passed the Immigration Act of 1924, barring further immigration by people of Asian descent—including Japanese. Moreover, even the economic argument for maintaining good relations with the Americans began to lose its force as Congress, in an effort to protect domestic industries, raised tariffs to unprecedented levels. By the end of the 1920s, therefore, Japan's economy was in the midst of a recession, and Japanese leaders assigned much of the blame to America, along with those in Japan who had advocated close relations with the United States.

The **zaibatsu** were massive industrial and financial conglomerates that emerged after the Meiji Restoration. Some, such as Mitsui and Sumitomo, were originally rice merchant firms during the Tokugawa period, while others, such as Mitsubishi and Yasuda, formed in the late nineteenth century. Although they possessed enormous economic and political power in early-twentieth-century Japan, they were generally owned by particular families.

Economic Distress and the Rise of Ultranationalism

A great deal changed in Japan in the 1930s. At the start of the decade the country's government was closer than it ever had been to a constitutional republic. Japan had a vibrant, democratically elected Diet, and since World War I had been governed by cabinets made up mostly of civilian politicians committed to trade, arms limitation, and cooperation with Great Britain and the United States. These steps toward democracy, however, began to unravel as the economy underwent a serious downturn in 1930. Signs of trouble appeared earlier, as the country's foreign trade, which had boomed during and immediately after the war, began to suffer as its major trading partners—particularly the United States—raised tariffs to record levels. In 1930 the Hamaguchi cabinet returned the yen to the gold standard, believing that this would demonstrate the country's commitment to a stable international economic order, and hence open Western markets once again to Japanese goods. However, the strategy caused the economy to contract, and unemployment to soar. To make matters worse, a bumper crop of rice that year—combined with a worldwide fall in the prices of agricultural commodities in general—resulted in a collapse in the price of rice. Much of the countryside fell into despair.

Some Japanese intellectuals reacted to the economic crisis by attacking capitalism itself and calling for Japan to follow the lead of Russia—by this time known as the Soviet Union—in embracing **Communism**. These, however, were a small minority, as most Japanese regarded Communism as entirely contrary to the nation's cherished traditions. Japanese communists, therefore, faced prosecution under the **Peace Preservation Act of 1925**, which made it a crime to advocate the abolition of private property or the overturning of Japan's national entity.

A more common line of attack came from officers of the army and navy, as well as those belonging to a host of **ultranationalist** organizations that sprang up during this period. Japan was suffering, they claimed, because it had been corrupted by Western ideas. Instead of following Japan's ancient traditions, which emphasized honor, harmony, selflessness, loyalty, and devotion to one's benefactors, too many Japanese had embraced the Western values of individualism, rationalism, and materialism. Particularly objectionable to such critics were the zaibatsu, Japan's major corporations, such as Mitsui, Mitsubishi, and Sumitomo. Guided only by their selfish interests and lust for money, the zaibatsu, the critics claimed, had brought ruin down upon the simple folk of the countryside. Moreover, the critics charged that the corporations were secretly controlling the government in Tokyo through their campaign contributions to political parties. Indeed, the parties themselves came under attack for being "un-Japanese" and undermining the natural unity of the country.

A number of strains of ultranationalism developed in the 1920s and 1930s, but most possessed a set of core beliefs, including those listed in the box "Core Beliefs of Japanese Ultranationalism." What Japan needed, argued the ultranationalists, was drastic reform in the name of the emperor; some even called for a Shōwa Restoration (Shōwa being the name given to the current emperor's reign), harkening back to the Meiji Restoration of the previous century. They called for the Diet and its political parties to be dissolved; the zaibatsu to be nationalized, the economy to be brought fully under government control, and the society to be purged of all Western influences. Only then could Japan return to its true principles.

CORE BELIEFS OF JAPANESE ULTRANATIONALISM

Traditional Confucianism

Originally imported from China, traditional Confucianism embraced the following ideas.

Filial Piety (*xiao*): The respect that children are expected to show toward their parents. This was supposed to serve as the model for subjects' obedience to their ruler and the submission of a wife to her husband. It also implied that the living possessed obligations to the dead, leading to the tradition of ancestor worship. All of this suggested the existence of a fixed, harmonious universe based on natural hierarchies, in which people were expected to understand and accept their places within the family and society as a whole. Confucian thinkers were inclined to criticize Westerners for valuing the material self-interest of individuals over their duty to others.

The Unity of Nature and Man (*tenjin-goitsu*): Held that every entity possessed a fixed nature (*li*) that was superior to its physical form. This principle particularly rejected Western science, which was at best irrelevant (in the sense that it could not understand what was of genuine importance, the *li*) and at worst disrespectful (in the sense that it, in the words of Carmen Blacker, treated nature "as a mere collection of playthings to be copied, measured and compared."[4]

Bushido

The term *Bushido* is not unproblematic, as historian Karl Friday has pointed out, since it came into vogue in the seventeenth and eighteenth centuries to describe a set of values that were supposed to have been held by the warrior (samurai) class during Japan's medieval period. However, the very writers who attempted to codify these principles (for example, Yamamoto Tsunetomo and Daidōji Yūzan) did so at a time when Japan was at peace and thus were invoking examples from the past in order to prepare samurai not for a life of warfare but for careers as administrators and bureaucrats. The concept was again revived during the Meiji period as a set of guidelines for all subjects of the emperor, not just for warriors. Nevertheless, Japan's leaders—particularly those in the military and the bureaucracy—took the following principles of Bushido extremely seriously.

Honor: Defined by Inazō Nitobe as "a vivid consciousness of personal dignity and worth."[5] Accompanying this was a keen sense of shame, a need to redeem oneself for one's mistakes, and a burning desire to avenge slights to oneself or to one's superiors.

Acceptance of Death: "The Way of the Samurai," Yamamoto Tsunetomo writes, "is found in death."[6] This was more than a simple willingness to face death but rather an enthusiasm for an honorable death. It certainly implied a selfless bravery in battle, but ultimately encouraged the practice of *seppuku* (ritual suicide by disembowelment) as a means of regaining lost honor.

Loyalty to Superiors: An extension of the Confucian concept of filial piety, involving a complete rejection of self. As Yamamoto writes, "being a retainer is nothing more than being a supporter of one's lord, entrusting matters of good and evil to him, and renouncing self-interest."[7] Such loyalty even takes precedence over traditional religion, since if the retainer "will only make his master first in importance . . . the gods and Buddhas will give their assent."

Self-Discipline: One must constantly monitor one's personal behavior, always avoiding carelessness. Studies, particularly in the ways of warfare, must be undertaken constantly. Great attention needs to be paid to personal appearance and actions, as all of these will contribute to or detract from one's reputation.

"No Mind": When faced with a momentous decision, it is best to act according to one's impulses. If one is truly self-disciplined, one will be prepared for any eventuality and will not need to think about how to respond. Those who hesitate, weighing the costs and benefits of different courses of action, are contemptible, because they are ultimately motivated by fear of death and desire for personal gain.

State Shintō

A combination of traditional religious beliefs about Japan and its origins and nationalism as imported from nineteenth-century Europe, state Shintō was promoted heavily by the Meiji authorities as a means of legitimating the new emperor-centered regime they established. While it failed to win a mass following at the time, ultranationalists vigorously asserted its principles in the 1930s. It commonly expressed itself in the form of devotion to the *kokutai*, which roughly translates as "national entity" (in other words, the social and political makeup of the nation) and included the following.

Worship of the *Tennō*: Translates only imperfectly into English as "worship of the emperor." However, no other monarch in the world could hold this title (other kings and emperors were called *kotei*), as it had not only political but religious significance. The Tennō was purported to be a descendant of Amaterasu, the sun goddess, and was therefore divine. This stands in contrast even to Chinese emperors, who were said to possess the so-called mandate of heaven, but never claimed to be gods.

Japan's Pan-Asian Mission: Japan was destined to expand, either by economic or military means (probably both), and to free East Asia from the clutches of Western imperialism, both in its Anglo-American (capitalist) form and its Soviet (communist) manifestation.

Sincerity: According to historian Richard Storry, nationalists believed that the "Japanese had a capacity for intuitive virtue unequalled by any other race." What mattered most was not any given act (such as, say, the invasion of China) but the motive behind it. So long as the Japanese acted with "sincerity of heart," and selfless devotion to the Tennō, they could do no wrong. By contrast, Europeans and Americans tended to be grasping and materialistic, their actions constantly tainted by self-interest.[8]

The Ultranationalists' Foreign Policy

The ultranationalist movement also argued for a new foreign policy, claiming that Japan had pursued the wrong path by looking to the West for inspiration. It had sought prosperity through foreign trade, particularly with the British and Americans, while turning a blind eye to European imperialism in East Asia. Such a course, the reformers argued, had left Japan dangerously dependent on those countries for vital imports and therefore unable to pursue a truly independent foreign policy. They denounced the naval limitation treaties that Tokyo had signed in the 1920s, which they alleged had forced Japan into a humiliating condition of inferiority at sea. Under pressure from these elements, the government announced in 1934 its intent to no longer be bound by those agreements, but it was imperative that the country never again be forced to accept such a humiliating position. ·

Pursuit of an independent foreign policy, the reformers claimed, required nothing less than self-sufficiency in the resources needed by Japan's industrial economy. Part of this could be accomplished through domestic reform; in a **planned economy**, organized for the common interest, reformist bureaucrats could ensure that resources were steered to their most productive purposes. But because Japan possessed few natural resources of its own, self-sufficiency also implied the ability to draw on resources outside the country. Fortunately, nearby lands abounded in commodities such as rubber, tin, iron ore, coal, and petroleum. Once the Japanese had guaranteed access to these resources—through military conquest if necessary—Japan would finally win the respect of the world.

> A **planned economy** is one in which the government makes the most critical decisions regarding prices, wages, the allocation of resources, and what to produce and in what quantities. The Soviet Union and Nazi Germany are probably the best examples of countries that operated planned economies, although in the 1930s many other countries experimented with economic planning, including the United States.

The only problem was that Western countries continued to dominate nearly the entire region. The British held India, Ceylon (modern-day Sri Lanka), Burma (Myanmar), Malaya, and Singapore, while the Dutch owned the oil-rich East Indies (Indonesia), the French controlled Indochina (Vietnam, Laos, and Kampuchea), the Americans held the Philippines, and the Soviet Union owned eastern Siberia and the northern half of Sakhalin Island. Even in China, supposedly an independent country, Americans and Europeans enjoyed "extraterritoriality"—that is, the privilege of being subject only to their home nations' laws even as they lived and worked in China. Moreover, the Chinese government was fighting a civil war against an insurgent Communist Party that received its orders from the Soviet Union. For the reformers, then, Japan's destiny lay in the pursuit of Pan-Asianism, liberating East Asia from the imperialists (both Western and Soviet) and uniting the region into what would eventually come to be called the Greater East Asia Co-Prosperity Sphere.

The Occupation of Manchuria, 1931

The first step toward a new order in East Asia came in Manchuria in 1931. Concluding that the corrupt party-dominated government would not act in defense of the national interest, officers of the Japanese Army stationed in southern Manchuria decided to take matters into their own hands. In September 1931, outside the town of Mukden, a small group of officers secretly blew up a length of track belonging to the Japanese-owned South Manchuria Railway. Then, after blaming the sabotage on Chinese "bandits," the Japanese Army moved to occupy all of Manchuria. Japan's civilian government had not authorized this operation, but after an unsuccessful attempt to restrain the army in Manchuria, the leaders in Tokyo decided to go along with it.

The Japanese invasion of Manchuria was a clear challenge to the U.S. Open Door Policy as well as a violation of several treaties that Tokyo had signed over the past decade. The international response, therefore, was one of alarm. Nevertheless, given that most of the industrialized world was in the grip of the Great Depression, no concrete steps were taken to block this act of aggression. U.S. Secretary of State Henry Stimson responded with a policy of "nonrecognition"—that is, he announced that the U.S. government would not accept the occupation as legitimate, but neither would it do anything to stop it. In late 1932 a commission formed by the **League of Nations** officially branded the occupation of Manchuria an act of aggression, but took no further action.

The **League of Nations** was formed by the United States and the other victorious powers after World War I. It was the world's first formal international organization committed to the maintenance of peace through arbitration and negotiation. By the early 1930s nearly all the world's major countries (aside from the United States and the Soviet Union) were members of the league.

The failure of the Western powers to intervene meant that Japan's military leaders believed they could proceed with their plans to pursue the ideal of pan-Asia without foreign interference. In March 1932 Tokyo announced its sponsorship of the new state of Manchukuo, to be ruled by the former Chinese emperor (who had been deposed twenty years earlier, at the age of five), although in practice he remained a puppet of the Japanese. That December the Japanese Army invaded the neighboring Chinese province of Jehol, which was promptly declared part of Manchukuo. The following year Japan withdrew its delegation from the League of Nations.

"Government by Assassination"

If the situation in China was rapidly growing dangerous, affairs in Japan itself were no less so, at least if one were inclined to oppose the ambitions of the militarists and ultranationalists. A series of plots were hatched in the 1930s to overthrow the existing government—always in the emperor's name—by assassinating prominent public figures such as zaibatsu executives, party leaders, diplomats who advocated friendship with the United States and Great Britain, and even army and navy officers who dared challenge the ambitions of the radicals. Some of these conspiracies were uncovered before they could be put into practice, but there were many successful assassinations during this period, and their victims included three Japanese prime ministers. Indeed, political murder had become such a common feature in the early to mid-1930s that a Canadian journalist described Japan's political structure as "government by assassination."

The most serious incident occurred on February 26, 1936, when several entire units of the Japanese Army, spurred on by radical young officers, attempted a coup d'état. In the early morning hours some 1,500 soldiers fanned out through Tokyo, targeting cabinet members, the Ministry of War, and the offices of the country's largest newspaper. The uprising was suppressed only after the Shōwa emperor took the practically unprecedented step of intervening personally. Even though the constitution gave him absolute power, the emperor traditionally was content to remain on the sidelines, allowing the prime minister and his cabinet to rule in his name. However, with the cabinet paralyzed—one member had been killed, while others were in hiding—and some leading generals expressing sympathy for the rebels, he ordered the army and navy to use force to restore order. Within hours the insurgents found themselves surrounded by 20,000 soldiers loyal to the government. Some of the ringleaders chose to commit suicide; the rest were taken into custody, although ultimately only 124 were prosecuted.

The defeat of the rebellion temporarily calmed the turbulent political climate in Tokyo, but it did nothing to undermine support for traditionalist and ultranationalist causes. Membership in organizations espousing these ideas continued to surge throughout the decade: by 1940 there were at least 1,000 such organizations in Japan, claiming a total membership of at least half a million people. Indeed, most of the ultranationalists' beliefs were enshrined in a publication called *Fundamentals of Our National Entity* (see p. 74 for excerpts). Drafted by a committee of university faculty and government officials, it was published in 1937, and the first printing of 300,000 was distributed to all of the nation's teachers. This short book credited Japan with a unique ability to "assimilate and sublimate" ideas from China and India, taking from them what was useful and discarding what was destructive. All of the recent instability in Japan, it claimed, had been the result of a failure to do the same with Western ideas. The Japanese had understood the value of Western industrial methods but had at the same time unthinkingly accepted Western individualism and rationalism—both of which were destructive to the kokutai. The country would truly succeed only once these dangerous notions had been eradicated.

The uprising also gave increased power to the army and navy. An old rule was reinstated requiring that all army and navy ministers be active-duty generals or admirals in their respective service branches. Although ostensibly intended to keep radicals out of the cabinet, the real effect was to grant the military services veto power over all cabinet decisions. The army or navy could at any time order the army or navy minister to resign and then refuse to appoint a successor, in which case the prime minister and his entire cabinet would be obligated to step down. From this point on it was the armed forces, and not civilian politicians, who effectively controlled the cabinet.

The "China Incident"

Meanwhile Japan's actions in foreign policy continued to raise concerns internationally. Fearing the spread of Soviet influence in East Asia, the government in November 1936 joined Nazi Germany in signing an agreement known as the

Anti-Comintern Pact, in which the two powers pledged to cooperate in resisting the spread of international Communism. More important, however, were ongoing efforts by Japan's government to create a Japanese-dominated "autonomous region" in China north of the Great Wall to serve as a buffer against possible Soviet expansion into East Asia.

Although Tokyo's ambitions caused alarm among many Chinese, for the first few years the Nationalist government at Nanjing showed little willingness to resist Japan's growing power in the country's northern provinces. Indeed, China's premier, Jiang Jieshi, seemed far more interested in fighting Chinese communists, who had established "Soviet republics" in several locations in the country. However, this all changed in December 1936, when Nanjing abruptly changed course and concluded an agreement with the communists; from now on, both sides pledged, they would cooperate against the common threat of Japanese imperialism.

Alarmed by this show of unity on the part of the Chinese, the government in Tokyo began preparations for war, and after fighting broke out at the Marco Polo Bridge, just outside Beijing, in July 1937 the Japanese Army launched a full-scale offensive. Within a few weeks the Japanese had captured the Chinese cities of Beijing, Tientsin, and Shanghai. By the end of the year the Japanese Army had seized the capital of Nanjing (followed by an orgy of looting, murder, and rape that shocked the world). Qingdao, Hankou, and the port cities of South China (the most important of which was Guangzhou) fell in 1938. Yet the Chinese government refused to surrender, moving its capital west to Chongqing, deep in the interior of the country.

Given the U.S. commitment to the Open Door, Japanese aggression in China could not help but attract attention from Washington. Initially the administration of Franklin D. Roosevelt offered no more than public condemnation of Japan's actions; in 1937 domestic affairs remained the president's highest priority.[9] However, the behavior of Japanese troops in the weeks after the fall of Nanjing outraged American public opinion. To make matters worse, Japanese aircraft attacked and sank a U.S. gunboat—the U.S.S. *Panay*—on the Yangtze River on December 12. Although Tokyo claimed it was an accident and promised to pay an indemnity, many Americans viewed it as an intentional act of war. All of this led the Roosevelt administration to become more involved in East Asian affairs, offering small amounts of military aid to Jiang Jieshi's government in exchange for a promise by Jiang not to yield to Japanese demands. Moreover, 1938 saw the beginning of a major expansion in the size of the U.S. Navy, which was the only force in the Pacific capable of taking on the Japanese fleet. Finally, in 1939 the administration announced that it would not renew its 1911 commercial treaty with Japan, thus holding out the possibility of economic sanctions if Tokyo did not abandon its designs on China.

Most Japanese leaders deeply resented what they saw as American interference in East Asia. Few considered their country's efforts in China to be an act of aggression; as official Japanese government spokesmen said again and again, they did not seek to take territory from China (aside from Manchuria), but rather wanted the Chinese government to become a junior partner with the Japanese to resist Soviet Communism and promote mutual economic development. According to this view, the Americans were merely trying to protect their own selfish commercial interests in China—unlike the Japanese, who claimed to have the true interests of China at heart. Besides, why should the United States have any particular say over what happened in East Asia? Americans had for years been using the Monroe Doctrine as a justification for intervening in the nations of Central and South America and for denying foreign powers any right to do likewise. Japan had never sought to challenge the Monroe Doctrine; why, then, should the United States not recognize Japan's Monroe Doctrine for Asia?

Political and Economic Changes

The ongoing war in China brought significant changes to Japan itself. A rising faction of reformist bureaucrats had long been calling for greater government control over the economy, and during wartime their voices became impossible to ignore, particularly since they enjoyed considerable support among the army as well. The formation in 1937 of the Cabinet Planning Board, charged with allocating imported raw materials, gave these bureaucrats a power base at the heart of the government. Their campaign for economic centralization culminated in the National General Mobilization Law of 1938, which, although it stopped short of nationalizing the zaibatsu, gave the cabinet virtually unlimited authority to regulate any aspect of Japan's economy and society.

But while the government's executive power grew exponentially in the late 1930s, its legislative branch—the Diet, the only organ of the national government to be elected democratically—became all but irrelevant. Under the Meiji Constitution of 1889 the cabinet had always been answerable only to the emperor, but during the 1910s and 1920s it had become common for cabinets to be selected from among the leadership of the country's leading political parties. By the second half of the 1930s, however, this practice had been all but abandoned, and cabinets fell under the control of generals, admirals, career bureaucrats, and court officials. One might hear the occasional criticism of government policy on the floor of the Diet, but even muted criticism of matters such as the "holy war" in China could invite assassination attempts in Tokyo's increasingly ultranationalist atmosphere. On the whole, the Diet had become by 1939 little more than a rubber stamp for decisions made by the cabinet.

Yet even if the Diet had continued to function as it had in the 1920s, it is unlikely that it would have exercised any sort of restraint over the cabinets of the time, as the public at large seemed equally intent on a policy of expansion. Radio broadcasting was entirely in government hands, while the newspapers had been subject to increasingly stringent censorship under the Peace Preservation Act of 1925. Throughout the 1930s, therefore, the public had been fed a steady ration of nationalist propaganda, while those voices who dared to challenge government policy were subject to harassment or worse.

The 1930s brought economic change as well. The Inukai cabinet pulled the yen from the gold standard in December 1931, and recovery began almost immediately. The country soon experienced a boom in the production of cotton textiles, as Japanese firms could import cotton from India at bargain prices, spin it into cloth in factories (which mostly employed daughters of peasant families and paid extremely low wages), and export it throughout East Asia. The conquest of Manchuria and much of eastern China provided these firms with reliable markets. True, the demands of the war required Japan to import huge quantities of oil, scrap iron and steel, and other materials from the United States—making the country dangerously dependent on such imports—but massive military spending gave a tremendous boost to heavy industry. The increase in spending on arms and munitions was gigantic. In 1931 less than a third of the government's budget went toward the army and navy; in 1940 such spending constituted 70 percent. Ironically, the main beneficiaries of these developments were the very zaibatsu that the nationalists and militarists claimed to despise; the four largest corporations by 1940 controlled nearly a quarter of all the capital in Japan.

JAPAN'S STRATEGIC DILEMMA IN 1940

While the economy was booming, the mood of the cabinet at the start of 1940 was somber. When the China Incident first broke out in 1937, army generals had confidently predicted victory within three months. While it was true that the army had won nearly every battle against the Chinese, success on the battlefield did nothing to bring the war to a conclusion. Tokyo was convinced that support from the outside—particularly from the Americans—was the only factor keeping Jiang Jieshi from agreeing to Japan's demands. But such an agreement was absolutely critical, for it was clear the Japanese Army lacked the troops to overrun a country as large as China. Indeed, by late 1938 there were not even enough men to impose an effective occupation over those parts of the country they had conquered, so that a powerful guerrilla movement was able to operate behind Japanese lines.

The irony in this massive commitment to the China Incident was that nobody in Japan had been particularly enthusiastic about fighting China in the first place. From Tokyo's perspective, Japan's efforts toward Pan-Asianism were as much in China's interests as they were in Japan's. Japanese leaders saw no good reason why Jiang Jieshi, who had a long established reputation as an anticommunist, would prefer to collaborate with Chinese communists rather than join Japan in ridding

East Asia of communist and imperialist influence. But by the end of 1939 the war had been going on for two and a half years and had cost more than 50,000 Japanese lives. The conflict was now about more than creating a new order in East Asia. The prestige of the Japanese Army was on the line; the sacrifices of its soldiers must not be in vain.

Developments outside China seemed no more promising. Relations with Great Britain and the United States continued to deteriorate as the war in China dragged on. On the Asian continent, Japanese and Soviet troops clashed outside the village of Nomonhan, near the border of Manchuria and Mongolia, in spring and summer 1939. What began in May as a skirmish escalated as both sides rushed reinforcements to the area, and by August more than 100,000 soldiers faced each other. The result was a serious reverse for the Japanese Army, which suffered some 17,000 killed and wounded. To make matters worse, in August, while the emperor's troops were fighting at Nomonhan, the German and Soviet governments announced they had concluded a nonaggression pact. Since Japan had only three years earlier signed an agreement with Hitler's regime, in which both sides committed to fighting the communist menace worldwide, Tokyo could regard this only as a betrayal.

Two events in the spring of 1940, however, offered some rays of hope. The first emerged in March, when Wang Jingwei, formerly an important figure in China's Nationalist government, announced that he had broken with Jiang Jieshi and was creating an alternative regime in Japanese-occupied Nanjing. Wang furthermore announced that if the Japanese agreed to recognize his regime as the legitimate government of China he stood prepared to sign a treaty with Japan that would include all of Tokyo's demands.

The second promising development occurred in Europe. War had broken out the previous September when Great Britain and France declared war on Nazi Germany in the wake of that country's invasion of Poland. Little actual fighting had taken place since the fall of Poland in October, but in April and May German forces quickly overran Denmark, Norway, the Netherlands, Belgium, and even France. Great Britain now stood alone, facing a German-dominated continent.

These German victories had profound implications for East Asia, since French, British, and Dutch colonies in the region suddenly appeared vulnerable. If Tokyo were to demand concessions in these areas—or, indeed, even chose to invade them—would their colonial masters be in any position to resist? The British, bowing to Japanese pressure, agreed to close the Burma Road, an important route by which U.S. and British aid had been reaching Jiang Jieshi. Perhaps now, some military leaders argued, there was an opportunity cut off Jiang's miserable regime from all of its sources of outside support and to win control of the rich resources of Southeast Asia, allowing Japan to resolve the China Incident once and for all!

Thus for the first time in months the global situation seemed to favor Japan. The only question was how the United States might respond to efforts by Tokyo to profit from Germany's victories in Europe. Although Japan's leaders deeply resented what they regarded as American meddling in East Asia, none of them in 1940 sought war with the United States. Even the most bellicose of the ultranationalists were calling for war against the British, the Dutch, and the Soviet Union, but not against America. Those few Japanese who had visited the United States were deeply impressed by the country's industrial power, which even in the midst of the Great Depression dwarfed that of Japan. In any war between Japan and the United States the outlook for Tokyo appeared grim. It would be much better if the Americans could be encouraged simply to accept Japanese leadership in East Asia, but how could this be done? Some believed that American fears could be allayed through careful diplomacy, including promises of a studious respect for U.S. interests in the region. Others, on the other hand, claimed that concessions would only fuel American arrogance and that it was best to attempt to deter the United States from interfering—perhaps through an alliance with Germany.

This, then, was Tokyo's dilemma in July 1940: should the country do whatever it takes to bring about victory in China, even at the cost of Japan's relations with the United States? Or should the country's goals in East Asia be sacrificed in the interest of getting along with the Americans? In this contest it was clear that the ultranationalists possessed the upper hand. The high command of the army embraced traditionalist ideas, almost to a man. Considerable numbers of ultranationalists could be found in the navy and bureaucracy as well, and there were even some among the emperor's closest advisers. Meanwhile, the state-controlled media provided a steady stream of ultranationalist propaganda to the people of Japan. While, as Storry points out, it would be erroneous to claim that all Japanese believed themselves to be descendants of the gods, "with few exceptions they were convinced they had a birthright envied but unrivalled by other nations of the world."[10]

On the other hand, some voices could still be heard resisting these trends. There were still suggestions that it was wiser to maintain friendly relations with the West, even if it meant backing away from the dream of Pan-Asianism. Even some believers in Pan-Asianism started to question whether the war in China was being carried out for the benefit of Asia in general or whether Japan was simply practicing its own form of imperialism. Regardless, it was becoming dangerous to espouse such ideas, at least publicly. The ultranationalists increasingly regarded pro-Western sentiments as insults to the kokutai, and they had again and again demonstrated their willingness to employ violence to avenge such insults.

PART 3: **THE GAME**

MAJOR ISSUES FOR DEBATE

- To what extent are Western ideas (rationalism, individualism, capitalism, etc.) compatible with Japanese tradition (Confucianism, Bushido, Shintō, etc.)

- Which is a better course in foreign affairs, a unilateral policy that emphasizes military action and economic self-sufficiency or a trade-based policy that stresses international cooperation?

- What should be regarded as Japan's greatest enemy, Western imperialism or Communism?

- Is the war in China being fought according to pan-Asianist principles? Or is Japan behaving more like an imperial power in East Asia?

- Does Pan-Asianism demand that Japan go to war?

- Does Bushido demand war in defense of national honor, even if there is a good chance that the nation in question will lose?

RULES AND PROCEDURES

How to Win

Victory is accomplished by satisfying the objectives listed in your role sheet and (if you are not an Indeterminate) your faction advisory. Many of those objectives reflect efforts to influence policy—for example, some characters seek to conclude an alliance with Germany, while others seek to prevent it; some want to reform Japan's economy, while others oppose this. Other objectives are personal—for example, many characters seek positions on the cabinet.

In general, players who have met more than two-thirds of their objectives will be declared the winners, and those meeting fewer than one-third are declared the losers. In addition, for some roles there is one final result that will result in an automatic loss.

The Cabinet, the Supreme Command, and the Imperial Court

Japan, 1941: Between Pan-Asianism and the West attempts to simulate the politics of Imperial Japan in 1940–41. The game encompasses the three main policy-making bodies: the cabinet, the Supreme Command, and the Imperial Court. Historically many initiatives would have also been submitted for approval to other bodies, such as the Diet and the Privy Council, but by 1940 these institutions had so declined in significance that they operated virtually as rubber stamps. They are not, therefore, represented in the game.

The **cabinet**, with the prime minister at its head, collectively determines the overall direction of government, reaching its decisions via consensus. Many countries today are run by cabinets, and normally their members are chosen by those elected to the national legislature. However, the Meiji Constitution (which served as Japan's governing document until after World War II) is modeled on the German Constitution of 1871, and although that constitution provides for an elected Diet, it has no formal authority over the cabinet. Japan's prime minister is appointed rather by the emperor and serves until or unless he resigns, the cabinet falls, or (less likely) the emperor chooses to dismiss him. It also includes the war minister, navy minister, foreign minister, president of the Cabinet Planning Board, and in larger games, home minister, finance minister, and commerce and industry minister. The holders of all these posts are selected by the prime minister, and they hold their positions until or unless they resign or the cabinet falls (as detailed later in the game book). The war minister *must* be an active-duty general, while the navy minister *must* be an active-duty admiral. Any character may hold the other cabinet posts.

At the start of the game Konoe has just recently been named prime minister, and has already selected most of his cabinet. The war minister is Tōjō Hideki, Oikawa Koshirō is navy minister,[11] and Hoshino Naoki is president of the Cabinet Planning Board. In larger games, Hiranuma Kiichirō begins as home minister, Kobayashi Ichizō as commerce and industry minister, and Ogura Masatsune as finance minister. Only the post of foreign minister remains to be filled, and Prime Minister Konoe is tasked with choosing a candidate by the end of Game Session 1.

The main function of the cabinet ministers is to submit petitions for consideration by the cabinet and, ultimately, by the emperor (although in practice the emperor cannot reject them; the most he can do is ask that they be reconsidered, which merely delays them.) Each petition may propose one or more specific actions. For example, a petition might be submitted proposing that Japan enter into an alliance with Germany or send a special envoy to the Dutch East Indies to demand a new trade agreement. Petitions are to be made in writing and circulated to all members of the class in advance of the Game Session during which the petition is to be discussed. Petitions may be drafted by any player, but only a cabinet minister may bring one before the full cabinet.

A cabinet remains in power until it falls, which happens if either of the following occurs: (1) the prime minister, for whatever reason, chooses to resign or (2) if any other cabinet minister resigns and no one can be found to take that minister's place. In practice this is likely to happen only in the case of the war and navy ministers, since the army or navy chief of staff may order the war or navy minister, respectively, to resign, and then refuse to allow a successor to be appointed.

The **Supreme Command** consists of four individuals—the chiefs of staff and vice chiefs of staff of the army and navy. (In smaller games there will be no vice chief of staff of the navy.) At the start of the game the army chief of staff is Sugiyama Hajime, the navy chief of staff is Prince Fushimi Hiroyasu (or, in smaller games, Nagano Osami), the army vice chief of staff is Tsukada Osamu, and the navy vice chief of staff (if there are enough players) is Kondō Nobutake. A chief of staff may not simultaneously serve on the cabinet in any capacity. The chiefs hold their positions until or unless they choose to resign or a majority of the members of their faction opt to replace them, in which case the members of the Imperial Court (speaking for the emperor) select their successors. Vice chiefs of staff serve at the pleasure of the chiefs, and may be replaced at any time. The Supreme Command, unlike members of the cabinet, may not submit petitions to be discussed at conferences and placed before the emperor, although they may draft such petitions in the hope that a cabinet member will submit them. More important, the chiefs of staff have the authority to order the war or navy minister to resign from the cabinet and to refuse to allow a successor to be appointed.

The emperor himself exists in the game only symbolically; he is represented by a photograph or some other image. The **Imperial Court** faction, meanwhile, collectively represents the emperor in all proceedings. This means that they are free to question the cabinet and Supreme Command on any petition that comes forward. They also possess a number of additional powers, some of which are routine functions, while others carry risks. The emperor, after all, traditionally does not intervene directly into the making of policy. This tradition need not be rigorously followed, but deviations could lead to ultranationalist violence against them, to "liberate" the emperor from his allegedly evil advisers. If this occurs, the object representing the Tennō is handed over to the ultranationalists, who then gain the power to determine and express the imperial will.

The routine functions of the emperor (as expressed by the president of the Privy Council and the lord keeper of the Privy Seal) are as follows:

- If a cabinet falls, the emperor chooses a new prime minister. Any player may be chosen, including a member of the court.

- If either the army or navy chief of staff resigns, or is removed by a vote of faction members, the emperor chooses a new one from among the appropriate faction (Army for army chief of staff, Navy for navy chief of staff).

- After making any appointment of a prime minister or military chief of staff, the emperor may give instructions *of a general nature* to the new appointee. These should not be direct orders (although these can be given, as detailed later in the game book, they are risky) but should rather be phrased as suggestions. For example, "Try to avoid war with America" is fine; "Do not attack the United States" is not.

- If the emperor is opposed to a proposal that the cabinet has approved, he may temporarily withhold the Imperial Sanction and ask the ministers to reconsider. However, if the cabinet refuses to change its mind, the proposal automatically receives the Imperial Sanction. In practice, in other words, the emperor cannot overturn cabinet decisions.

- If a character has been arrested and/or put on trial, the emperor may pardon him.

Starting with Game Session 2, the emperor may, **once per Game Session**, grant *kazoku* (noble status) to any character for a particularly effective speech or some other service. A grant of kazoku counts toward that character's victory objectives at the end of the game. For example, if a character has achieved four out of the seven victory objectives listed on his or her role sheet, plus has been awarded kazoku, that player may count five objectives as satisfied.

The following functions are constitutionally permitted to the emperor (again, expressed through the Imperial Court), but historically were very rarely used. They may be exercised in the game, but only with great caution, for they tend to make the emperor responsible, and therefore culpable, for potentially controversial decisions.

- If a cabinet is in danger of falling due to the resignation of a cabinet minister, the emperor may refuse to accept that minister's resignation for the remainder of that session. In this instance the requirement of unanimity among cabinet ministers is, in effect, waived. Any petition that is considered by the cabinet during the remainder of that conference is accepted if it has the support of a majority of the members of the cabinet.

- The emperor, as supreme commander of the armed forces, may issue a direct order to the army and/or navy, either authorizing them to do something without cabinet approval or (more likely) to cease and desist from doing something contrary to the cabinet's wishes.

- The emperor may, in extreme cases, demand the resignation of a cabinet minister, or even dissolve the cabinet by calling for the resignation of the prime minister. If, for some reason, a new cabinet cannot be formed, the emperor may then rule by decree.

Imperial Conferences

With the exception of Game Session 1, in which two candidates for the cabinet position of foreign minister will "audition" for the post, each session represents an Imperial Conference. Although all players attend each Imperial Conference, not all may speak freely. All players must be provided in advance with copies of all petitions to the emperor that are to be considered during the next Game Session.

The arrangement of the room is critical to conveying the relative importance of the participants. At the absolute front of the room, if possible on a dais or in a raised chair, sit the members of the Imperial Court. Whatever symbolic image or object being used to represent the person of the emperor should be placed close to them. In front of them, and facing them, members of the cabinet and the Supreme Command sit in chairs arranged in a semicircle, with the prime minister occupying the central position. Behind them sit all of the other players.

It is the job of the prime minister to preside over the conference, which primarily means deciding the order in which petitions will be considered as well as how much time is spent in deliberating on each petition. He begins by bowing (see p. 47) in the direction of the symbolic representation of the emperor, then asking a member of the cabinet who wishes to present a petition to the emperor to speak briefly about it. Each person who speaks is expected to begin by bowing to the symbolic representation of the emperor. Anyone who fails to do so is certain to be chastised—or worse—for lack of respect!

After a petition has been presented, discussion begins. Again, the prime minister presides, but discussion among cabinet ministers, the president of the Privy Council, the lord keeper of the Privy Seal, and the Supreme Command should take place along largely informal, freewheeling lines. Other players may speak, but must raise their hands and wait to be acknowledged by the prime minister.

The goal of the discussion is for the cabinet ministers to reach a *unanimous* decision—to accept, to accept in amended form, or to reject—regarding each petition under consideration at the conference. The essence of Japanese politics was consensus; no decision was to be associated with a particular individual but was to be reached jointly, so that Japan's leadership bore collective responsibility for its choices.

In the game, this form of consensus politics is represented as follows. At any point in the discussion of a petition the prime minister may take an informal poll of cabinet members (the army and navy chiefs of staff, while they may participate in the discussions, do not vote). Those who find themselves in a minority on the question are expected either to change their votes to agree with the majority (indeed, anyone who chooses this should be prepared to speak and write in defense of the majority's decision) or to resign. The prime minister must demand that a cabinet minister step down if he does not do one or the other.

While the army and navy chiefs of staff are not polled, they may choose to disrupt the proceedings at this point demanding that the war or navy minister resign from the cabinet—and then, presumably, not allowing a successor to be chosen, so that the cabinet falls.

NOTE

Only the prime minister; president of the Cabinet Planning Board; and the war, navy, and foreign ministers vote on petitions related to foreign or military affairs. Home, commerce and industry, and finance ministers, if in the game, may freely comment on such petitions, but do not vote on them.

If a cabinet minister resigns in the midst of a conference, a recess is immediately called while the prime minister attempts to find a replacement. The Gamemaster will place a definite time limit on this, depending on how much class time remains and how much there is left to discuss at the conference. If the prime minister fails to fill the vacancy within the allotted time, he must step down—this means that the entire cabinet has fallen. In this case, another recess is called, once again with a time limit to be determined by the Gamemaster, in which the members of the Imperial Court select a new prime minister, who in turn selects new cabinet ministers. Note that former cabinet ministers, including those who belonged to the cabinet that has just fallen, may be reappointed, assuming that they are willing to serve. Also, a prime minister may choose to name himself to additional positions in his own cabinet, subject to the requirements for war and navy ministers (i.e., the former must be an active-duty general with support from the army chief of staff and the latter, an active-duty admiral with the backing of the navy chief of staff).

<aside>
NOTE

The emperor may, in extreme circumstances, refuse to accept the resignation of a cabinet minister, thus allowing the cabinet to continue its deliberations.
</aside>

As soon as a petition has received unanimous acceptance by the cabinet, the members of the Imperial Court must decide whether to grant the Imperial Sanction to the petition (meaning that the emperor formally ratifies it) or to ask that the cabinet reconsider. If they choose the latter, the members of the cabinet immediately take a new vote on the measure; as before, the decision must be unanimous—those who dissent from the majority's decision must change their minds, resign, or be dismissed from their positions (with the understanding that this may well cause the cabinet to fall). If the cabinet accepts the petition a second time, then the Imperial Sanction *must* be granted.

Once a petition has been either rejected by the cabinet or approved and granted the Imperial Sanction, the conference proceeds to the next petition on the agenda. Petitions that are not taken up or decided on during a conference for reasons of time are *not* automatically placed on the agenda for the next conference. The decision as to what petitions are to be considered at a conference always lies with the prime minister.

Bowing

To this day, bowing remains integral to social interactions between Japanese people. It is as natural as shaking hands when Westerners greet and interact with one another. It is integral to Japanese culture to the degree that one still bows even when speaking to someone on the telephone. It is that reflexive.

Westernization and modernization have eroded bowing etiquette in contemporary Japan, and many Japanese today do not bow well, but the game is set in 1940, and there is a groundswell of support for traditional Japanese culture, so bowing is very much in order. Today, a nodded head may substitute for a bow in

You might want to add a greeting to your bow. Consider the following:

Good afternoon: *konichiwa* (Koh-NEE-chee-wa)

Good-bye: *sayonara* (Sy-OH-nah-rah)

Thank you: *arigatou* (Ah-REE-gah-toh)

informal situations, but this game consists of a series of cabinet meetings, which are clearly *formal* occasions, so bowing is absolutely required.

When bowing, it is important to understand your place in the social hierarchy. For example, players should bow more deeply and longer to those who outrank them. And, of course, everyone must show the utmost respect for the emperor, who is assumed to be constantly present in Game Sessions 2–6. Remember that bowing is serious business. Clowning around and bowing too deeply or ostentatiously long, might very well be regarded as a sign of disrespect for the person being bowed to.

In terms of the game, the object representing the emperor has the highest rank. Everyone should bow toward it at the beginning and end of each session. The members of the Imperial Court, in terms of honor, rank just below the emperor, and thus deserve long bows from everyone, including cabinet ministers. The prime minister is the highest ranking minister, and other cabinet ministers possess higher ranks than those who are not in the cabinet.

But this is complicated because the army and navy did not regard civilians—even cabinet ministers—as equals, unless they were members of the Imperial Court (in which case they bore some element of the emperor's majesty). They should express this by giving no more than cursory bows to civilians. In addition, the chiefs of staff outrank other military officials regardless of their standing in the cabinet.

The deepness of your bow combines a number of factors. It shows your respect for the person you are bowing to, it signals the sort of social interaction you are having, and it indicates the distance between your social standings. Here are some guidelines:

Bow 15 degrees: For a casual greeting to an equal.

Bow 30 degrees: To thank someone, like a customer or a superior.

Bow 45 degrees: To express deep gratitude, respectful greeting, or formal apology to a superior.

Bow 90 degrees: To show respect to the emperor.

Men should keep their hands at their sides, and their palms should be flat and against their legs. Women should keep their hands together on their thighs with the fingers of their right hand over the left. Since all the roles in the game are men, female players may choose which way they want to comport themselves. Everyone should keep the eyes down when bowing.

Regarding meetings: For the Japanese *on time* is *late*.

Materials Mobilization Plans

On two occasions during the game—Game Sessions 2 and 6 (the first and fifth Imperial Conferences)—the president of the Cabinet Planning Board is expected to submit a Materials Mobilization Plan. Historically, this plan was an annual survey of all of the resources that were likely to be produced in the Japanese Empire as well as what could be imported from abroad, along with a breakdown of how these resources would be allocated during the course of the next fiscal year. Since certain resources (especially steel and oil) were in such short supply, these plans were generally matters of strenuous debate, as various groups in Japan put forward their claims.

In the game, the Materials Mobilization Plan is handled abstractly. In submitting a plan, the president of the Cabinet Planning Board simply proposes that one of four areas receives priority. These areas are army munitions, navy munitions, expansion of productive capacity (new factories, mines, etc.), and production of consumer goods.

The cabinet may choose to accept the plan as proposed by the president of the Planning Board or may amend it. However, a plan *must* be approved during the second and fifth conferences. Also, unlike other matters that come before the cabinet, Materials Mobilization Plans *do not* require the Imperial Sanction.

The result of the first plan (for 1941, considered in Game Session 2) will affect developments later in the game. If the army is given priority, the army receives a bonus when it fights against the Chinese or the Soviets, while if the navy has priority, it receives a bonus in fighting the British, Dutch, or Americans. If priority goes to expansion of industrial capacity, there can be *two* equal priorities in the 1942 Materials Mobilization Plan (considered in Game Session 6). If it goes toward production of consumer goods, civilian morale improves, and Japan will receive a bonus in negotiating trade treaties.

Negotiating with Foreign Powers

Much of the game involves Japan's relations with foreign governments and there are several avenues by which negotiations may occur. In larger classes, certain players will be assigned the roles of the U.S. and German ambassadors. They are credentialed to speak for their governments, although in certain instances—for example, the conclusion of a treaty—they will need to get permission from their home countries. Also, U.S. diplomats may enter the game later. In the absence of either of these options, the Gamemaster is assumed to represent all foreign governments.

The "China Incident"

The period during which the game takes place was one that saw almost continuous fighting between Japanese and Chinese forces in Asia. The day-to-day conduct of the China Incident is not dictated by the cabinet but rather by the army. Once each session the army chief of staff may call for a vote of all of the members of his faction, either during the session or in a meeting outside of class. If a majority agree to do so, an offensive in China is launched simply by informing the Gamemaster of their intent. The Gamemaster will then determine the outcome of the offensive by rolling dice. Successful operations may bring Jiang Jieshi closer to making peace on Japan's terms. However, unsuccessful ones will undermine the overall effectiveness of the army. Whatever the result, the army chief of staff must report it to the cabinet during the next session.

Insubordination by the Armed Forces

During the 1930s the army and navy were both notorious for their willingness to act independently of the cabinet, even defying cabinet decisions they did not like. At the end of each conference the army and navy chiefs of staff will have the option of carrying out initiatives without cabinet authorization. They may also refuse to carry out certain actions authorized by the cabinet. Once a decision is made, the only thing that can prevent the army or navy from ignoring or defying the cabinet is a direct order from the emperor, but for the Imperial Court to do so would involve potentially great risks (see the powers of the Imperial Court on p. 44.)

In addition, there are any number of aggressive young army officers in Manchuria and China who are eager for action. If they feel that the leadership in Tokyo is being too timid, there is a chance they might take matters into their own hands, perhaps even causing an international incident.

Assassinations

Ultranationalist organizations remained highly active throughout the period covered in the game, and numerous assassination plots were hatched against Japanese political and business leaders who seemed too friendly to the West or to Western ideas. Some characters in the game will have connections to ultranationalist groups and may order assassination attempts against others. A player authorizing such an attempt informs the Gamemaster of his or her intent; the Gamemaster ultimately decides whether to allow it, based on the persuasiveness of the ultranationalist's argument as well as the circumstances of the game. If the attempt is allowed, the Gamemaster rolls a die to determine the result, which is then announced to the entire group. The attempt may either succeed or fail; either way there is a chance the identity of the person ordering the assassination is revealed.

Arrests

If a character is implicated in an assassination attempt, or a character in the game accuses another character of breaking the law, then the home minister (if the class is large enough to have one) decides whether the state will pursue criminal charges. If there is no home minister, then the prime minister may decide. In either case, if criminal charges are filed, the defendant is arrested and put on trial (see Trial Procedures, in the following section).

Trial Procedures

If a player is arrested, as a result of an assassination attempt or by decision of the cabinet, that player will be put on trial during the next Game Session. (Trials for those arrested during the final Game Session take place at the end of that session.) A player on trial has an opportunity to explain in a speech why his or her actions were justified, while anyone seeking to punish the player may offer oral testimony for the prosecution. Afterward the result of the trial is determined by the Gamemaster through the roll of a die. If the Gamemaster judges any speech to be particularly strong or weak, he or she may choose to modify the die roll for or against the defendant. (It is assumed that the prosecution has—through fair means or foul—amassed enough evidence to convict, so the trial is more a rhetorical exercise than anything else.)

Trials end in a number of possible outcomes. A defendant might be executed by hanging (a highly dishonorable means of death), ordered to commit seppuku (more honorable, but still death), sentenced to a prison term (forcing the defendant to remain silent for one or more Game Sessions), or acquitted.

A majority of the Imperial Court—speaking for the emperor—have the option of pardoning anyone, either before or after a trial (see the emperor's functions on p. 44).

BASIC OUTLINE OF THE GAME

Although the specific game schedule will be determined by the Gamemaster, *Japan, 1941: Between Pan-Asianism and the West* normally begins with one or more setup sessions, involving lecture or discussion of the historical background, game rules, and primary source documents. The game itself consists of a series of meetings. The first of these will consist of an "audition" in which two candidates vying for the position of foreign minister will express their overall views of what course Japan should take in foreign policy. Others are then encouraged to offer ideas on the subject, and at the end Prime Minister Konoe will decide which candidate will be invited to join the cabinet.

Subsequent Game Sessions will represent Imperial Conferences, in which the cabinet, Supreme Command, and Imperial Court take up various issues related to Japan's foreign, domestic, and military policy. Ultimately they are likely to be faced with critical decisions regarding war and peace.

The final Game Session will be followed by one or more debriefing sessions in which the players—now out of character—discuss what happened in the game, and how in-game developments compared with the actual historical record.

SETUP SESSION 1

The Gamemaster (GM) introduces the historical setting and game rules. The GM distributes the reading quiz.

Assignments

- *Before the class begins:* Read Parts 1–4 of the game book (pp. 00–00)

- *For the next class:* Read the Core Texts reprinted in the game book (pp. 00–00)

SETUP SESSION 2

The GM leads discussion of Bushido and the conflict between traditional Japanese culture and that of the West. At end of class, the GM distributes individual role sheets and faction advisories.

Assignments for Next Class

- Read the Core Texts reprinted in the game book (pp. 00–00)

- Read your role sheet and faction advisory

- Complete the reading quiz

SETUP SESSION 3

The GM leads discussion of Pan-Asianism. The GM collects the reading quiz.

Assignments for Next Class

- Read the supplemental documents reprinted in the game book (pp. 00–00)

- Prepare essays or speeches for Game Session 1

GAME BEGINS

GAME SESSION 1

Format and date: faction meetings and tea ceremony, July 1940
Session leader: prime minister
First half of Game Session: faction meetings to discuss ideas, assignments, and strategy
Second half of Game Session: traditional Japanese tea ceremony, at which Tōgō Shigenori and Matsuoka Yōsuke, who are auditioning for the position of foreign minister, discuss competing visions of Japan's role in world affairs

Assignment for Next Class

- Prepare essays or speeches for Game Session 2

GAME SESSION 2

Format and date: Imperial Conference, summer/autumn 1940
Session leader: prime minister
Subjects for discussion may include

- Japanese membership in the Tripartite Pact

- Occupation of north Indochina

- Recognition of Wang Jingwei's government

- Materials Mobilization Plan for 1941

Assignments for Next Class

- Read the supplemental documents reprinted in the game book (pp. 00–00)

- Prepare essays or speeches for Game Session 3

Format and date: Imperial Conference, spring 1941
Session leader: prime minister
Subjects for discussion may include

- The Imperial Rule Assistance Association

- The "New Economic Order"

- The "Draft Understanding" from the embassy in Washington

Assignment for Next Class:

- Prepare essays or speeches for Game Session 4

Format and date: Imperial Conference, summer 1941
Session leader: prime minister
Subjects for discussion may include

- The latest message from the United States

- War against the Soviet Union

- Occupation of southern Indochina

- A trade agreement with the Dutch East Indies

Assignment for Next Class

- Prepare essays or speeches for Game Session 5

GAME SESSION 5

Format and date: Imperial Conference, autumn 1941
Session leader: prime minister
Subjects for discussion may include

- Japan's economic situation

- Terms of further negotiation with United States

- Preparations for war

Assignment for Next Class

- Prepare essays or speeches for Game Session 6

GAME SESSION 6

Format and date: Imperial Conference, November 1941
Session leader: prime minister
Subjects for discussion may include

- War against the United States and Great Britain

- Materials Mobilization Plan for 1942

Assignment for Next Class

- Read "What Happened in History?" (distributed by the GM at the end of class)

DEBRIEFING SESSION

Led by: instructor
Format: In this session, your instructor will lead a discussion of the game, revealing who won and exposing any secrets as well as contemplating which side, from our modern viewpoint, was in the "right." The instructor will also compare events in the game with what really happened and cover the history of Japan in 1940–41 and the outbreak of the "Greater East Asia War."

ASSIGNMENTS

Normally instructors will require a certain amount of writing as part of the game, although the form that this writing takes will depend on the instructions in each character's role sheet. All papers are to be written *in character* and should draw on the ideas expressed in the course readings, but their subjects will vary widely. Papers will generally take one of the following forms, although others are possible with the approval of the Gamemaster:

- A petition to be considered by the cabinet and, if approved, submitted to the emperor. Each petition should propose and present an argument for a specific course of action, either in foreign or domestic policy. The petition is due *before* the session in which you intend the cabinet to consider it.

- A speech given either in support of or in opposition to a petition that will be brought before the cabinet. Speeches are due *before* the session in which the petition is being considered.

- A statement offered for or against a defendant in a trial, written either by the defendant or someone else. For example, it might be a defense of someone implicated in an assassination, demonstrating that the defendant was merely following the proper principles of Bushido. Depending on how convincing the Gamemaster finds this appeal, he or she may award a bonus or penalty to the die roll to determine the defendant's fate. Such statements must be submitted *before* the session in which the trial is to take place.

- An ambassador will be required to make regular reports to his home government, informing it of recent developments. Note that as players in the game, ambassadors will be privy to information that they never would have had historically. Reports, therefore, should not contain specific details that an ambassador would not have known. For instance, a report from the British ambassador announcing that Japan is about to invade Southeast Asia would not be permitted. However, it would be appropriate to write about something that Japan has already done, drawing on the tenor of cabinet discussions for insight as to why Tokyo has decided on such a course.

- If Ogata Taketora is in the game, players may wish to contribute editorials to the newspaper *Asahi Shimbun*. Ogata is instructed to prepare two editorial sections, one for Game Session 3 and the other for Game Session 5.

- A diary entry giving the player's impression of the events going on in Tokyo during this period. These may be turned in at any point in the game.

Students are also expected to participate in the game by speaking—that is, by making speeches before the cabinet (these should be delivered, *not* read), becoming involved in debates, or negotiating and strategizing (to the extent that the Gamemaster is aware of these activities). The Gamemaster may also wish to give a slight grade advantage to those who win, and/or a slight disadvantage to the grades of those who lose.

COUNTERFACTUALS

Politics in prewar Japan was highly confusing, involving multiple bodies, and jurisdiction was often unclear. While the emperor, the cabinet, and the Supreme Command were the most important institutions, the Diet and the Privy Council usually had a say in matters. Moreover, the tradition of collective responsibility made it almost impossible to attribute particular policies to specific individuals. Equally uncertain was the role of the emperor, who on paper seemed to have limitless authority but who—again, by tradition—exercised it subtly and with considerable restraint.

In an effort to make the game playable, the political system has been simplified. As a result, there are a few counterfactuals. First, the Diet and Privy Council are not represented. Although the Diet had played a critical role in politics in the 1910s and 1920s, by 1940–41 it had become quite weak and was generally incapable of blocking anything that the cabinet wanted. Indeed, the most critical questions of foreign policy, which lie at the heart of this game, were not subject to any official oversight by the Diet, although individual Diet members were known to express strong opinions on international affairs. The Privy Council, meanwhile, was made up of the emperor's closest advisers and is represented in the game by Kido Kōichi, lord keeper of the Privy Seal.

Likewise, certain individuals who were historically involved in decision making in Japan in 1940–41 have been left out, either because they were involved for only a brief period or because the points of view they expressed were already represented by more important figures. For example, until October 1940 the actual army chief of staff was Prince Kan'in Kotohito, who retired and was replaced by Sugiyama Hajime. However, since their views were practically identical, Prince Kan'in is not represented in the game.

The Imperial Conference, which forms the heart of the game, is also something of a counterfactual. It actually simulates two important phenomena in imperial Japanese politics—Liaison Conferences and Imperial Conferences. The former were historically attended by the most important cabinet members as well as by the Supreme Command; these meetings were instituted in 1940 so that any conflict between the two bodies could be resolved without triggering a cabinet crisis. It was here that the most critical decisions were made. Imperial Conferences also consisted of the Supreme Command and key cabinet members, plus the emperor and the president of the Privy Council (one of the emperor's key advisers). These, however, were largely ceremonial affairs in which the cabinet formally presented petitions to the emperor. For the sake of time, however, the two conferences are combined into a single event, in which cabinet, Supreme Command, and Imperial Court all participate.

While in the game any matter may be discussed at an Imperial Conference, historically this would not have been the case. Military strategy, for example, was entirely in the hands of the Supreme Command, and while the cabinet might discuss the possibility of war with another power, it never would have addressed the best way to wage war. The inclusion of such matters in the deliberations for the game serves to add depth to the discussion.

Finally, the role of the emperor is abstracted, to represent the fact that while his power was theoretically unlimited, his range of action was strictly limited by tradition.

4

Most of the players will belong to one of three factions representing the most important interest groups in Japanese politics in 1940–41. It is to be expected that, in most instances, members of factions will have similar goals. However, this is not always the case. Ultimately players must follow the directions in their individual role sheets, even if this places them at odds with other members of their faction.

Army

The army is the most influential organization in Japanese politics and society. Founded during the earliest days of the Meiji Restoration, it was a force made up largely of peasant conscripts, armed with rifles, drilled in European tactics, and commanded by samurai. This army fought for the Meiji Emperor and scored victory after victory in a sixteen-month civil war against forces loyal to Tokugawa Yoshinobu, Japan's last shōgun. The army takes great pride in its connection to the imperial institution as well as its dedication to the principles of Bushido, and it has enhanced its prestige through significant victories in the Sino-Japanese War of 1894–95, the Russo-Japanese War of 1904–05, and the Great War of 1914–18 as well as the current ongoing China Incident. However, the army has recently encountered some potentially dangerous setbacks. Although it claims control over a massive stretch of territory in China, in reality it is dreadfully overextended. Moreover, in 1939 it suffered a humiliating defeat at the hands of the Soviet Army at Nomonhan. The generals, therefore, have become touchy about their military reputation, and for that reason are determined that there will be no retreat from China short of total victory.

The following characters belong to the Army faction, although not every character may be represented in the game you're playing:

As a young officer in 1922, General **Sugiyama Hajime** was the first head of the Japanese Army Air Service. After the outbreak of the China Incident he became commander of the North China Area Army and later was placed in charge of the Yasukuni Shrine in Tokyo. He was appointed army chief of staff earlier this year.

Nicknamed *Kamisori* (razor) for his sharp mind, General **Tōjō Hideki** served as chief of staff of the Kwantung Army in Manchuria and later as inspector-general of army aviation. As the game begins, he has just been named minister of war in the Konoe cabinet.

Lieutenant General **Suzuki Teiichi** is chief of the Political Affairs Bureau of the Asia Development Board and is recognized as an expert on economic planning. In the present cabinet he serves as a "minister without portfolio"—that is, without a particular ministry to oversee, or even a formal vote, but as an adviser on economic matters.

Formerly commandant of the Japanese Army War College and chief of staff of the Central China Area Army, Lieutenant General **Tsukada Osamu**, currently holds the post of army vice chief of staff.

Major General **Muto Akira**, served in a number of capacities with the army in China, before returning to Tokyo in 1939 to take up the post of chief of the Military Affairs Bureau of the War Ministry. He is known to exercise considerable influence behind the scenes.

Imperial Court

The Imperial Court consists of the emperor's most trusted advisers. Originally these were the *genrō*, elder statesmen who had guided Japan through its period of rapid modernization after the Meiji Restoration. By 1940 all of the original genrō are dead, but the emperor continues to rely on the advice of the men closest to him. The primary function of this group is to represent the interests of the emperor. In this game no single individual plays the emperor; rather the Tennō is represented abstractly, through a photograph, perhaps, or a chrysanthemum, or some other symbolic object. As holders of this object, the members of the court have the collective right to determine the emperor's will and to speak with the emperor's voice. The court's overriding concern in the game is to insulate the emperor from the consequences of national humiliation or defeat.

The following characters are members of the Imperial Court, although not every character may be represented in the game you're playing:

Hara Yoshimichi is regarded as one of Japan's foremost legal scholars, having long served as a law professor at Tokyo Imperial University. In the late 1920s he was minister of Justice in the cabinet of Tanaka Giichi and soon afterward was named to the Privy Council, a group of twenty-four of the emperor's closest advisers. He became president of the council earlier in 1940, succeeding Konoe Fumimaro (who resigned to become prime minister).

Prince **Konoe Fumimaro** is, next to the emperor himself, the country's best-known political leader, having served as president of the House of Peers, president of the Privy Council, and now prime minister—for the second time. When he resigned from that post last year, it was because he was tired of being a "robot" for the army. Will this time be any different?

Prince **Fushimi Hiroyasu**[12] is the emperor's first cousin. He has spent nearly his entire career in the navy and, in 1922, was promoted to admiral. A longtime advocate of naval expansion, he harshly criticized the naval limitation treaties that Japan signed in the 1920s. Since 1932 he has been chief of the Navy General Staff, but is believed to be considering retirement.

Baron **Hiranuma Kiichirō** in the mid-1920s founded an organization called the *Kokuhonsha* (National Foundation Society), committed to defending Japan's traditional national polity (*kokutai*) from all foreign ideologies, such as socialism, anarchism, and democracy. In 1939 he briefly served as prime minister, and as an elder statesman (*jōshin*) he continues to exert considerable influence. He has just been tapped as home minister in the Konoe Cabinet.

Marquis **Kido Kōichi** is scion of one of Japan's greatest noble families and has spent his entire career in government service, having held multiple cabinet positions. He has just been appointed Lord Keeper of the Privy Seal, the emperor's closest adviser.

Navy

The Navy was founded in 1871, after the Meiji Restoration. Since Japan lacked an indigenous naval tradition, it patterned itself largely after the navies of Great Britain and the United States. For this reason, it stood for years in the shadow of the army, and indeed, to this day it is less powerful politically than its rival branch of the service. Nevertheless, the navy gained tremendous prestige after the Battle of Tsushima Straits (1905), in which the Russian Baltic Sea Fleet was annihilated in the waters separating Japan from Korea. Today the officer corps of the navy tends to attract young men from the best families, who regard it as more glamorous and refined than the army. Since the 1920s the Navy has regarded the United States as its most likely adversary, but the admirals view the possibility of a war against America with considerable ambivalence. At the moment Japan has the strongest naval presence in the Pacific, but that could change rapidly given America's vast industrial capacity. If there is a war, therefore, the navy is intent on firing the first shot. Only by winning a decisive battle at the start, the admirals believe, does Japan stand any chance of victory.

The Navy faction includes the following characters, although not every character may be represented in the game you're playing:

Admiral **Nagano Osami** has served in nearly every important capacity of the Imperial Navy, including navy minister and commander-in-chief of the Combined Fleet, the navy's main oceangoing force. He now serves on the Supreme War Council, but it is widely believed that he is angling to succeed Prince Fushimi as navy chief of staff.[13]

Admiral **Oikawa Koshirō**, formerly commander of Japan's main naval base at Yokosuka, was Konoe's pick for navy minister. His rise in the navy seems odd, given that he was a defender of the naval limitation treaties that Japan signed in the 1920s—treaties that most of the navy resisted. It is rumored that the secret of his success is his personal friendship with the emperor.

Admiral **Shimada Shigetarō** succeeded Oikawa earlier this year as commander of the Yokosuka Naval District. He is the rare case of a high-ranking naval officer who never publicly took a side in the debates over the naval disarmament treaties of the 1920s. He is believed to be looking toward a formal cabinet position.

Prince **Fushimi Hiroyasu** (see description on p. 61).

During the early days of the China Incident, Vice Admiral **Kondō Nobutake** commanded a group of cruisers and destroyers charged with covering the landing of Japanese troops in southern China. His success in that capacity led to his appointment as vice chief of staff under Prince Fushimi.

Vice Admiral **Toyoda Teijirō** is vice navy minister. His promising career suffered in the early 1930s, when his support for naval limitation treaties proved unpopular among his fellow navy officers. However, an impressive performance as director of a naval aircraft factory in Hiroshima turned things around, and since 1935 he has held a series of important offices, including commander of the Imperial Japanese Air Service.

Rear Admiral **Oka Takasumi** had a distinguished career in the submarine service of the Imperial Navy before being named chief of the Naval Affairs Bureau of the Navy Ministry. In this capacity he is known to exercise a great deal of power from behind the scenes.

Vice Admiral **Itō Seiichi** has commanded virtually every kind of surface warship, from light cruiser through battleship. In 1938 he was named chief of staff of the navy's Second Fleet, which saw action off the coast of China. Now he has a desk job, serving as the Navy Ministry's chief of personnel. Might he be angling for a more prestigious post?

Indeterminates

Players who are not members of the Army, Imperial Court, or Navy factions take on the role of Indeterminates. This does not mean that they lack strong opinions; merely that they are unaffiliated the other factions and therefore have more independence. Many of the independents are business executives or civilian bureaucrats serving in the various ministries of the Japanese government. Others are ambassadors from the United States and Germany, while still others are influential Japanese journalists.

Among the Indeterminates are the following characters, although not every character may be represented in the game you're playing:

Matsuoka Yōsuke spent ten years of his youth in the United States, earning a degree from the University of Oregon. Once back in Japan he first served in the Foreign Ministry, then embarked on a political career as a member of the Imperial Diet. In 1935 he was named president of the South Manchuria Railway Company. Now that Prince Konoe is prime minister, he is being talked about as a potential foreign minister.

Hoshino Naoki is a career bureaucrat who spent much of the 1930s as vice minister for industrial development, leading a team of bureaucrats to Japan's newly established client state of Manchukuo. In recognition of his skill in economic planning, Prince Konoe has named him president of the Cabinet Planning Board.

Tōgō Shigenori has had a long and distinguished career in the foreign service, most recently as ambassador to the Soviet Union, where he helped negotiate a cease-fire in the fighting around Nomonhan in 1939. Before that he served as ambassador to Germany. Today is he considered a leading candidate for the post of foreign minister in Prince Konoe's newly formed cabinet.

Joseph Grew has been U.S. ambassador to Japan since 1932. While the United States is not particularly well liked in Tokyo these days, Grew is personally popular among the country's ruling elite, and he and his wife are regulars on the capital's social scene. Can he help smooth over relations between the two powers?

Kobayashi Ichizō is one of Japan's most successful businessmen, owning an inter-urban railway line, a department store, a zoo, a theater (featuring a very popular all-female musical troupe), an amusement park, a baseball team (the Hankyu Braves), and Japan's leading motion picture company. No doubt it was his great business acumen that led Prince Konoe to invite him to join his cabinet as minister of commerce and industry.

Kishi Nobusuke in 1935 was appointed deputy minister of industrial development for the state of Manchukuo, tasked with establishing a series of state-directed industries. His apparent success caught the eye of Prince Konoe, who named him vice minister of commerce and industry in his new cabinet. A man of Kishi's vast ambition is unlikely to wish to remain in that position for long, however.

Ozaki Hotsumi is an author and freelance journalist, widely regarded as an expert on Sino-Japanese relations. Prince Konoe was so impressed with his work that he invited him to join his "Breakfast Club," a close-knit group of personal advisers. Now that Konoe is prime minister, Ozaki's advice on China (as well as other subjects) will be more important than ever.

Sakonji Seizō, a former naval officer, was forced out of active duty for his outspoken support of the naval limitation treaties that Japan had signed in the 1920s. However, he soon found a lucrative position as president of the North Sakhalin Oil Company, which seeks to extract oil from territory leased from the Soviet Union. His work often brings him to Tokyo, where he is regarded as something of an expert on Soviet Russia.

In 1934 **Eugen Ott** was named military attaché to the German embassy in Tokyo; when the ambassador died in 1938 Ott was appointed to replace him. The Nazi government has made no secret of its desire to conclude an alliance with Japan, and Ott can be expected to press hard for this.

Ogura Masatsune for more than forty years was an executive for Sumitomo, one of the largest, and the oldest (dating back to 1615) of Japan's zaibatsu. In 1930 he became the company's general director (essentially the chief operating officer). He recently retired to pursue a career in public service, and Prince Konoe invited him to join his cabinet as minister of finance.

Kaya Okinori was a career bureaucrat with long experience in the Ministry of Finance and the Manchurian Affairs Bureau and briefly served as minister of finance in 1937. The following year he was named president of the North China Development Company, a state-financed subsidiary of the South Manchuria Railway Company. He is believed to be seeking a return to politics.

Immediately upon graduation from college, **Ogata Taketora** took a job at the Tokyo office of the *Asahi Shimbun*, one of Japan's largest and most influential newspapers. In 1928 he became the paper's executive editor, a position he has held ever since, guiding the newspaper through an especially challenging time in Japan's history.

Tanabe Harumichi has a long history in Japan's bureaucracy, in both the Communications Ministry and the Home Ministry; he even briefly served as governor of Osaka before being named vice chairman to the Privy Council of the newly established Manchukuo Empire. Tanabe is a longtime political ally of Baron Hiranuma Kiichiro (see p. 62); in August 1939 Hiranuma secured Tanabe a seat in the House of Peers. Now that Hiranuma is home minister, Tanabe may have other opportunities as well.

PART 5: **CORE TEXTS**

Selected Passages on Bushido

The following have been taken from a variety of sources, mostly written in the seventeenth and eighteenth centuries. They are likely to be particularly helpful to members of the Army and Navy factions, as they are called on to live up to the ideals of Bushido.

Sources vary throughout this edited collection of passages: see parenthetical notes after each excerpt.

ON DEATH

The Way of the Samurai is found in death. When it comes to either/or, there is only the quick choice of death. It is not particularly difficult. Be determined and advance. To say that dying without reaching one's aim is to die a dog's death is the frivolous way of sophisticates. When pressed with the choice of life or death, it is not necessary to gain one's aim. (Yamamoto Tsunetomo, *Hagakure: The Book of the Samurai*, trans. William Scott Wilson [Boston: Shambhala Publications, 2012], p. 3)

Above all, the Way of the Samurai should be in being aware that you do not know what is going to happen next. [. . .] Victory and defeat are matters of the temporary force of circumstances. The way of avoiding shame is different. It is simply in death. (*Hagakure*, p. 16)

In constantly hardening one's resolution to die in battle, deliberately becoming as one already dead, and working at one's job and dealing with military affairs, there should be no shame. But when the time comes, a person will be shamed if he is not conscious of these things even in his dreams, and rather passes his days in self-interest and self-indulgence. And if he thinks that this is not shameful, and feels that nothing else matters as long as he is comfortable, then his dissipate and discourteous actions will be repeatedly regrettable. (*Hagakure*, p. 19)

Calculating people are contemptible. The reason for this is that calculation deals with loss and pain, and the loss and gain mind never stops. Death is considered loss and life is considered gain. Thus, death is something that such a person does not care for, and he is contemptible. (*Hagakure*, p. 31)

Lord Naoshige said, "The Way of the Samurai is in desperateness. Ten men or more cannot kill such a man. Common sense will not accomplish great things. Simply become insane and desperate." (*Hagakure*, p. 31)

ON DETERMINATION

Among the maxims on Lord Naoshige's wall there was this one: "Matters of great concern should be treated lightly." Master Ittei commented, "Matters of small concern should be treated seriously." Among one's affairs there should not be more than two or three matters of what one could call great concern. If these are deliberated upon during ordinary times, they can be understood. Thinking about things previously and then handling them lightly when the time comes is what this is all about. To face an event anew solve it lightly is difficult if you are not resolved beforehand, and there will always be uncertainty in hitting your mark. However, if the foundation is laid previously, you can think of the saying, "Matters of great concern should be treated lightly," as your own basis for action. (*Hagakure*, p. 13)

When your mind is going hither and thither, discrimination will never be brought to a conclusion. With an intense, fresh and undelaying spirit, one will make his judgments within the space of seven breaths. It is a matter of being determined and having the spirit to break right through to the other side. (*Hagakure*, p. 34)

No matter what it is, there is nothing that cannot be done. If one manifests the determination, he can move heaven and earth as he pleases. [. . .] Moving heaven and earth without putting forth effort is simply a matter of concentration. (*Hagakure*, p. 37)

When one has made a decision to kill a person, even if it will be very difficult to succeed by advancing straight ahead, it will not do to think about going at it in a long roundabout way. One's heart may slacken, he may miss his chance, and by and large there will be no success. The Way of the Samurai is one of immediacy, and it is best to dash in headlong. (*Hagakure*, p. 47)

ON BRAVERY IN BATTLE

When on the battlefield, if you try not to let others take the lead and have the sole intention of breaking into the enemy lines, then you will not fall behind others, your mind will become fierce, and you will manifest martial valor. This fact has been passed down by the elders. Furthermore, if you are slain in battle, you should be resolved to have your corpse facing the enemy. (*Hagakure*, p. 39)

The phrase, "Win first, fight later," can be summed up in two words, "Win beforehand." The resourcefulness of times of peace is the military preparation for times of war. With five hundred allies one can defeat an enemy force of ten thousand. (*Hagakure*, p. 143)

One should not consider evading an important battle just because of its enormity. Nor should one advocate a battle that should not be fought on account of its being unexacting. (Shiba Yoshimasa, "The Chikubasho," in *Ideals of the Samurai: Writings of Japanese Warriors*, trans. William Scott Wilson [Santa Clarita, CA: Ohara Publications, 1982], p. 55)

In connection with military matters, one must never say that something can absolutely not be done. By this, the limitations of one's heart will be exposed. ("The Recorded Words of Asakura Soteki," in *Ideals of the Samurai*, p. 83)

When heading for the front, one should not be even a day behind the commander. There is a saying of the ancients that goes, "It is painful to hear the gong commanding a retreat, but a joy to hear the one that announces an advance." (Takeda Nobushige, "Opinions in Ninety-Nine Articles," in *Ideals of the Samurai*, p. 106)

When facing opposing forces, one should attack the place that has not yet been secured. There is a saying of the ancients that goes, "The man who defeats the enemy often is he who does not win by means of formation." There is another saying that goes, "It is the custom of our clan to simply dash in at full speed, and give the enemy no respite." ("Opinions in Ninety-Nine Articles," p. 106)

One should not praise the vastness or strength of the enemy in front of others. In the *San Lueh* it says, "One should not allow a man to speak of the good points of the enemy." ("Opinions in Ninety-Nine Articles," p. 107)

When one would make a surprise attack on the enemy, he should avoid the major roads and seek out the lesser ones. Then attack. An old proverb says, "When easily seen, one should take the by-paths; when not easily seen, the whole army may be moved." ("Opinions in Ninety-Nine Articles," p. 107)

Even if the enemy's forces are vast, one should attack if their defenses have been neglected. Moreover, one should think carefully before attacking a well-defended enemy, even though his force may be small. In the Sun Tzu it says, "One should not attack an imposingly defended camp, nor should he try to obstruct the flag of a well-arranged attack. To strike at such a force, one should keep in mind the suddenness of the snake of Mt. Ch'ang. When its head is struck, the tail comes forth; when the tail is struck, the head comes forth; when its middle is struck, both head and tail are at its attacker. There is a method of attacking such an enemy." ("Opinions in Ninety-Nine Articles," p. 110)

ON HONOR AND SHAME

Lord Naoshige said, "An ancestor's good or evil can be determined by the conduct of his descendants.'" A descendant should act in a way that will manifest the good in his ancestor and not the bad. This is filial piety. (*Hagakure*, p. 48)

[A] man whose profession is the use of arms should think and then act upon not only his own fame, but also that of his descendants. He should not scandalize his name forever by holding his one and only life too dear. On the other hand, in the light of this, to consider this life that is given to us only once as nothing more than dust and ashes, and lose it at a time when one should not, would be to gain a reputation that is not worth mentioning. One's main purpose in throwing away his life is to do so either for the sake of the Emperor or in some great undertaking of a military general. It is that exactly that will be the greatest fame of one's descendants. ("The Chikubasho," p. 47)

ON PERSONAL BEHAVIOR

It is because a samurai has correct manners that he is admired. (*Hagakure*, p. 17)

At a glance, every individual's own measure of dignity is manifested just as it is. There is dignity in personal appearance. There is dignity in a calm aspect. There is dignity in a paucity of words. There is dignity in flawlessness of manners. There is dignity in solemn behavior. And there is dignity in deep insight and a clear perspective. (*Hagakure*, p. 65)

One should not use rough manners with anyone. [. . .] It is said in the Li Chi that, "One is safe when polite, but in danger when ill-mannered." ("Opinions in Ninety-Nine Articles," p. 102)

ON LOYALTY

A man is a good retainer to the extent that he earnestly places importance in his master. This is the highest sort of retainer. If one is born into a prominent family that goes back for generations, it is sufficient to deeply consider the matter of obligation to one's ancestors, to lay down one's body and mind, and to earnestly esteem one's master. It is further good fortune if, more than this, one has wisdom and talent and can use them appropriately. But even a person who is good for nothing and exceedingly clumsy will be a reliable retainer if only he has the determination to think earnestly of his master. Having only wisdom and talent is the lowest tier of usefulness. (*Hagakure*, p. 4)

Being a retainer is nothing other than being a supporter of one's lord, entrusting matters of good and evil to him, and renouncing self-interest. If there are but two or three men of this type, the fief will be secure. (*Hagakure*, p. 6)

Every morning one should first do reverence to his master and parents and then to his patron deities and guardian Buddhas. If he will only make his master first in importance, his parents will rejoice and the gods and Buddhas will give their assent. For a warrior there is nothing other than thinking of his master. If one creates this resolution within himself, he will always be mindful of the master's person and will not depart from him even for a moment. (*Hagakure*, p. 9)

Concerning martial valor, merit lies more in dying for one's master than in striking down the enemy. (*Hagakure*, p. 42)

One must never be perfidious to his master. In the *Lun Yu* it says, "One should act according to the Way even in times of haste. One should act according to the Way even in times of danger." It says further, "When one is serving his master, he should exert himself." ("Opinions in Ninety-Nine Articles," p. 101)

In matters both great and small, one should not turn his back on his master's commands. In the Lun Yu it says, "Water will conform to the shape of the vessel that contains it, whether it be round or square." ("Opinions in Ninety-Nine Articles," p. 103)

ON SINCERITY

Lies and insincerity are unbecoming. This is because they are for self-profit. (*Hagakure*, p. 40)

When various reports are being given, one should not allow the least bit of distortion in terms of their truth or falsehood. If one hears that an official has put his own profit to the fore, he should be strictly ordered to the proper punishment. ("The Seventeen Articles of Asakura Toshikage," in *Ideals of the Samurai*, p. 70)

No matter how lacking a man may be in humanity, if he would be a warrior, he should first of all tell no lies. It is also basic that he be not the least bit suspicious, that he habitually stand on integrity, and that he know a sense of shame. The reason being that when a man who has formerly told lies and acted suspiciously participates in some great event, he will be pointed at behind his back and neither his allies nor his enemies will believe in him, regardless of how reasonable his words may be. One should be very prudent about this. ("The Recorded Words of Asakura Soteki," p. 83)

One should not tell a lie in any situation whatsoever. In the oracles of the gods it has been said, "Although truth may not be rewarded at once, in the end it will receive the compassion of the gods and Buddhas." In battle, however, shouldn't one act according to the circumstances of the moment? In the *Sun Tzu* it says, "Avoid the enemy's strength, strike at his weakness." ("Opinions in Ninety-Nine Articles," p. 102)

ON SELF-CONTROL

Narutomi Hyogo said, "What is called winning is defeating one's allies. Defeating one's allies is defeating oneself, and defeating oneself is vigorously overcoming one's own body." (*Hagakure*, p. 87)

There is nothing more base than for a man to lose his temper too often. No matter how angry one becomes, his first thought should be to pacify his mind and come to a clear understanding of the situation at hand. Then, if he is in the right, to become angry is correct. ("The Chikubasho," p. 53)

ON REVENGE

A certain person was brought to shame because he did not take revenge. The way of revenge lies in simply forcing one's way into a place and being cut down. There is no shame in this. By thinking that you must complete the job you will run out of time. By considering things like how many men the enemy has, time piles up; in the end you will give up. (*Hagakure*, p. 29)

No matter if the enemy has thousands of men, there is fulfillment in simply standing them off and being determined to cut them all down, starting from one end. You will finish the greater part of it. (*Hagakure*, p. 15)

* * *

Even if it seems certain that you will lose, retaliate. Neither wisdom nor technique has a place in this. A real man does not think of victory or defeat. He plunges recklessly towards an irrational death. (*Hagakure*, p. 16)

* * *

Even if one's head were to be suddenly cut off, he should be able to do one more action with certainty. [. . .] With martial valor, if one becomes like a revengeful ghost and shows great determination, though his head is cut off, he should not die. (*Hagakure*, p. 60)

ON *SEPPUKU*

If one felt that [. . .] [his] failure were a mortification, it would be the least he could do to cut open his stomach, rather than live on in shame with a burning in his breast and the feeling that he had no place to go, and, as his luck as a warrior had run out, he was no longer able to function quickly and had been given a bad name. But if one regretted losing his life and reasoned that he should live because such a death would be useless, then for the next five, ten or twenty years of his life, he would be pointed at from behind and covered with shame. After his death his corpse would be smeared with disgrace, his guiltless descendants would receive his dishonor for having been born in his line, his ancestors' name would be dragged down, and all the members of his family would be blemished. Such circumstances are truly regrettable. (*Hagakure*, pp. 58–59)

Imperial Rescript to Soldiers and Sailors, 1882

In the 1870s the Meiji government eliminated the privileges of the samurai class and created a new army and navy based on conscripted (mostly peasant) soldiers and sailors. The samurai fought back in the Satsuma Rebellion of 1877, but the insurgency was crushed after eight months of fighting. The uprising convinced Meiji leaders that the nation's armed forces had to be both insulated from politics and absolutely loyal to the emperor. In January 1882, therefore, the Meiji Emperor issued the Imperial Rescript to Soldiers and Sailors. This document, which all armed forces personnel were required to memorize, instructed the men of the army and navy to follow the code of Bushido, which had previously been an expectation only of the samurai class.

SOURCE: *Imperial Precepts to the Soldiers and Sailors and the "Boshin" Imperial Rescript* (Tokyo: Department of Education, 1913).

Soldiers and Sailors, We are your supreme Commander-in-Chief. Our relations with your will be most intimate when We rely upon you as Our limbs and you look up to Us as your head. Whether We are able to guard the Empire, and so prove Ourself worthy of Heaven's blessings and repay the benevolence of Our Ancestors, depends upon the faithful discharge of your duties as soldiers and sailors. If the majesty and power of Our Empire be impaired, do you share with Us the sorrow; if the glory of Our arms shine resplendent, We will share with you the honor. If you all do your duty, and being one with Us in spirit do your utmost for the protection of the state, Our people will long enjoy the blessings of peace, and the might and dignity of Our Empire will shine in the world. As We thus expect much of you, Soldiers and Sailors, We give you the following precepts:

1. The soldier and sailor should consider loyalty their essential duty. Who that is born in this land can be wanting in the spirit of grateful service to it? No soldier or sailor, especially, can be considered efficient unless this spirit be strong within him. A soldier or a sailor in whom this spirit is not strong, however skilled in art or proficient in science, is a mere puppet; and a body of soldiers or sailors wanting in loyalty, however well ordered and disciplined it may be, is in an emergency no better than a rabble. Remember that, as the protection of the state and the maintenance of its power depend upon the strength of its arms, the growth or decline of this strength must affect the nation's destiny for good or for evil; therefore neither be led astray by current opinions nor meddle in politics, but with single heart fulfill your essential duty of loyalty, and bear in mind that duty is weightier than a mountain, while death is lighter than a feather. Never by failing in moral principle fall into disgrace and bring dishonor upon your name. [. . .]

* * *

3. The soldier and the sailor should esteem valor. [. . .] To be incited by mere impetuosity to violent action cannot be called true valor. The soldier and the sailor should have sound discrimination of right and wrong, cultivate self-possession, and form their plans with deliberation. Never to despise an inferior enemy or fear a superior, but to do one's duty as soldier or sailor— this is true valor. Those who thus appreciate true valor should in their daily intercourse set gentleness first and aim to win the love and esteem of others. If you affect valor and act with violence, the world will in the end detest you and look upon you as wild beasts. Of this you should take heed.

4. The soldier and the sailor should highly value faithfulness and righteousness. [. . .] Faithfulness implies the keeping of one's word, and righteousness the fulfillment of one's duty. If then you wish to be faithful and righteous in anything, you must carefully consider at the outset whether you can accomplish it or not. If you thoughtlessly agree to do something that is

vague in its nature and bind yourself to unwise obligations, and then try to prove yourself faithful and righteous, you may find yourself in great straits from which there is no escape. [. . .] Ever since ancient times there have been repeated instances of great men and heroes who, overwhelmed by misfortune, have perished and left a tarnished name to posterity, simply because in their effort to be faithful in small matters they failed to discern right and wrong with reference to fundamental principles, or because, losing sight of the true path of public duty, they kept faith in private relations. You should, then, take serious warning by these examples.

5. The soldier and sailor should make simplicity their aim. If you do not make simplicity your aim, you will become effeminate and frivolous and acquire fondness for luxurious and extravagant ways; you will finally grow selfish and sordid and sink to the last degree of baseness, so that neither loyalty nor valor will avail to save you from the contempt of the world.

These five articles should not be disregarded even for a moment by soldiers and sailors. Now for putting them into practice, the all important thing is sincerity. These five articles are the soul of Our soldiers and sailors, and sincerity is the soul of these articles. If the heart be not sincere, words and deeds, however good, are all mere outward show and can avail nothing. If only the heart be sincere, anything can be accomplished. Moreover these five articles are the "Grand Way" of Heaven and earth and the universal law of humanity, easy to observe and to practice. If you, Soldiers and Sailors, in obedience to Our instruction, will observe and practice these principles and fulfil your duty of grateful service to the country, it will be a source of joy, not to Ourself alone, but to all the people of Japan.

From Fundamentals of Our National Entity [*Kokutai No Hongi*]

The ideology of Shintō ultranationalism was articulated in this book, first published in March 1937. Historian Walter Skya describes it as "a kind of state religious document addressed to all Japanese subjects that was designed to guide them in matters of religious faith and government." The first printing of 300,000 copies was distributed to all teachers, from elementary through university levels. Further editions were issued regularly for the next six years, and it is estimated that nearly 2 million copies were sold overall. Furthermore, it was supplemented by numerous commentaries written by Japan's intellectual elite to help ordinary people to understand its more subtle arguments.

Authorship of Kokutai no Hongi *is somewhat unclear. A first draft was completed in the mid-1930s by Hisamatsu Shin'ichi, a professor at Tokyo Imperial University and a renowned scholar of classical Japanese literature. However, before publication it was substantially rewritten twice: the first time by a committee of experts, and the second by Itō Enkichi, chief of the Education Ministry's Bureau of Thought Control. If Hisamatsu's postwar testimony is to be believed, he did not approve of these changes, but no copy of his original draft exists today.*

Note the use of the term National Entity. *Later translations have preferred the term* National Polity, *but the two may be used interchangeably.*

SOURCE: *Robert King Hall, ed.,* Kokutai no Hongi: Cardinal Principles of the National Entity of Japan; *trans. John Owen Gauntlett (Cambridge: Harvard University Press, 1949), pp. 51–55, 61, 63, 66–67, 75–77, 79–83, 85–95, 97–102, 130, 132–34, 138–45, 150, 157, 159, 161–62, 164–67, 169–72, 175–83.*

INTRODUCTION

Present-Day Japan and Her Ideologies

The book begins on a note of optimism. Japan is unique in its ability to draw on foreign ideas and incorporate only what is most useful about them and not allowing them to threaten the ancient order.

Our country faces a very bright future, blessed with a well-being that is indeed magnificent and with a very lively development abroad. Her industries are lively; her way of life has grown richer; and the progress made in the cultural fields merits attention. From of old, Oriental culture, which finds its origin in China and India, found its way into our country and was sublimated and fused into our "god-handed" national structure. And since the days of Meiji and Taishō, the various phases of our civilization have made remarkable strides through the introduction of modern European and American civilization. [. . .]

Through the great achievements of the Meiji Restoration, the people broke away from their old abuses, freed themselves of the feudal fetters, carried out their plans, and played their parts. Since then seventy years have passed, bringing with the lapse of time the realization of the great functions which we witness today.

Nevertheless, when we look back quietly on these great functions, there was by no means tranquility or rest, but immeasurable disquiet within and without, many difficulties in the path of advance, and much turmoil in the house of prosperity. In other words, the fundamental principles of our national entity tended to defy clarification. In the fields of scholastic pursuits, education, politics, economics, as well as in all fields of national life, there existed many defects. [. . .] The brilliant culture, too, came to have within it elements of richness and of foulness. And thus are brought into being various and knotty problems. At this time when our country is about to make great strides, light and shadow seem to have appeared before us hand in hand. However, this offers us nothing but a chance for advancement and a time for progress; so that we must grasp the real situation as it is at this time, both in and outside the country, must clarify the course we should follow together, must stir ourselves to find a way out of these difficult times, and must contribute all the more toward the development of our national destiny.

The authors come to the crux of the problem—that Western ideologies have been only half digested, thanks to having been consumed too quickly. Particularly dangerous are the ideas of individual liberty and equality; these are wholly contrary to the Japanese way.

The various ideological and social evils of present-day Japan are the fruits of ignoring the fundamentals and of running into the trivial, of lack in sound judgment, and of failure to digest things thoroughly; and this is due to the fact that since the days of Meiji so many aspects of European and American culture, systems, and learning, have been imported, and that, too rapidly. As a matter of fact, foreign ideologies imported into our country are in the main the ideologies of enlightenment that have come down since the eighteenth century, or their extensions. The views of the world and of life that form the basis of these ideologies are those of rationalism[1] and positivism[2], lacking in historical views, which on the one hand lay the highest value on, and assert the liberty and equality of, individuals, and on the other hand lay value on a world that is by nature abstract, transcending nations and races. Consequently, importance is laid upon human beings and their gatherings, which have become isolated from historical entireties, abstract and independent of each other. It is political, social, moral, and pedagogical theories based on such views of the world and of life that have, on the one hand made contributions to the various reforms seen in our country, and on the other have had deep and wide influence on our nation's primary ideology and culture.

The movement for enlightenment in our country began with the importation of the ideology of free rights of the people, which is the political philosophy of the period of enlightenment in France, and was followed by the introduction of such things as British and American conceptions of parliamentary politics, materialism[3], utilitarianism[4], and German nationalism; and efforts were made to carry out reforms in our bigoted habits and institutions. Such a movement, under the name of civilization and

---

1. *Rationalism is the belief that one's actions should be guided solely by reason and knowledge rather than by emotion or religious faith.*

2. *Positivism is the belief that no statement can be valid unless it can be verified either scientifically or logically.*

3. *Materialism is the belief that nothing exists that cannot be proven scientifically to have the characteristics of matter or energy.*

4. *Utilitarianism is a philosophical doctrine that holds that the best course of action is the one that accomplishes the greatest amount of good for the largest number of people.*

enlightenment, was a marked trend of the times, and brought into being the so-called Age of Europeanization, by influencing politics, economics, concepts, and customs. There arose, however, a movement in the face of it for return to tradition. This was a movement carried out in the name of the preservation of national virtues, and was a manifestation of national consciousness against the tide of the surging importation of European culture. And indeed this was because there was danger of extreme Europeanization doing injury to our national tradition and corrupting the national spirit running through our history. This brought about a pitting of one against the other, of Europeanism and the principle of preservation of national traits, so that concepts became confused, the people being bewildered as to what to follow—national tradition, or new foreign ideas. But with the promulgation in 1890 of the Imperial Rescript on Education,[5] the people came to discern the things accomplished by the Imperial Founder and Ancestors in the planting of virtues at the time of the founding of the nation, and herein they found a sure direction along which they should go. Nevertheless, in spite of the fact that this great Way based on this national entity was clearly manifested, foreign ideologies which remained as yet undigested led the fashion even in the days following, because importation of European civilization remained lively. In short, the concept of foreign individualism came in afresh and under a new ensign as positivism and as naturalism. Prior to and following this importation, idealistic concepts and scholastic theories were also brought in; and this was followed by the introduction of democracy, socialism, anarchism, communism, etc., and recent days saw the importation of Fascism; so that today we have reached a point where there has arisen an ideological and social confusion with which we are faced and wherein there has sprung up a fundamental awakening in regard to our national entity.

Consciousness of Our National Entity

The authors trace the problems of the modern West to individualism. Even many in the West have begun to recognize this, and the result has been the rise of totalitarian ideologies such as Nazism.

Paradoxical and extreme conceptions, such as socialism, anarchism, and communism, are all based in the final analyses on individualism, which is the root of modern Occidental ideologies, and are no more than varied forms of their expressions. In the Occident, too, where individualism forms the basis of their ideas, they have, when it comes to communism, been unable to adopt it; so that now they are about to do away with their traditional individualism, which has led to the rise of totalitarianism and nationalism and incidentally to the emergence of Fascism and Nazism. That is, it can be said that both in the Occident and in our country the deadlock of individualism has led alike to a season of ideological and social confusion and crisis. We shall

---

5. *Issued by the Meiji Emperor in October 1890, the* Imperial Rescript on Education *called for schools to embrace Western science and technology while emphasizing the uniqueness of Japan's* kokutai, *based on the bond between the divine emperor and his subjects.*

leave aside for a while the question of finding a way out of the present deadlock, for, as far as it concerns our country, we must return to the standpoint peculiar to our country, clarify our immortal national entity, sweep aside everything in the way of adulation, bring into being our original condition, and at the same time rid ourselves of bigotry, and strive all the more to take in and sublimate Occidental culture; for we should give to basic things their proper place, giving due weight to minor things, and should build up a sagacious and worthy Japan. This means that the present conflict seen in our people's ideas, the unrest in their modes of life, the confused state of their civilization, can be put right only by a thorough investigation by us of the intrinsic nature of Occidental ideologies and by grasping the true meaning of our national entity. Then, too, this should be done not only for the sake of our nation but for the sake of the entire human race, which is struggling to find a way out of the deadlock with which individualism is faced. Herein lies our grave cosmopolitan mission. It is for this reason that we have compiled the Fundamentals of the National Entity of Japan, to trace clearly the genesis of the nation's foundation, to define its great spirit, to set forth clearly at the same time the features the national entity has manifested in history, and to provide the present generation with an elucidation of the matter, and thus to awaken the people's consciousness and their efforts.

BOOK I: THE NATIONAL ENTITY OF JAPAN

The authors offer a brief account of Japan's early history (most of which has been redacted in the interest of brevity), emphasizing the divine origins of the nation and the institution of the emperor. Japan, they assert, is sacred, and the emperor a direct descendant of the sun goddess, Amaterasu Ōmikami.

I. The Founding of the Nation

The unbroken line of Emperors, receiving the Oracle of the Founder of the Nation, reigns eternally over the Japanese Empire. This is our eternal and immutable national entity. Thus, founded on this great principle, all the people, united as one great family nation in heart and obeying the Imperial Will, enhance indeed the beautiful virtues of loyalty and filial piety. This is the glory of our national entity. This national entity is the eternal and unchanging basis of our nation and shines resplendent throughout our history. Moreover, its solidarity is proportionate to the growth of the nation and is, together with heaven and earth, without end. We must, to begin with, know with what active brilliance this fountainhead shines within the reality of the founding of our nation.

Beginning of Heaven and Earth

Our nation was founded when its Founder, Amaterasu Ōmikami (Heavenly-Shining-Great-August-Deity), handed the Oracle to her Imperial Grandson Ninigi no Mikoto and descended to Mizuho no Kuni (Land of Fresh Rice-ears) at

Toyoashihara (Rich Reed-plain). And in relating the facts of the founding of our Land by the Founder of our Empire, the *Kojiki* and the *Nihon-shoki*[6] tell first of all of the beginning of heaven and earth, and of the making and consolidating. [. . .]

It is in this manner that the great principle touching the relationship between sovereign and subject was made manifest and our national entity established. Thus it is, too, that the descendants of Amaterasu ōmikami, the great reigning deity, descended to this Mizuho no Kuni, and that the prosperity of their Throne is together with heaven and earth without end. The great principle of the nation's beginning, therefore, is made manifest eternally and immutably [. . .], through the advent of the Imperial Grandchild. [. . .]

The Line of Emperors Unbroken for Ages Eternal

The authors contend that the superiority of Japan's national entity is most clearly seen in the fact that the line of emperors has been unbroken through history. In other countries rulers owe their positions to the acts of individuals, either their own or those of others. By contrast, the Japanese system is literally divine in origin and nature.

The Imperial Throne is the Throne of a line of Emperors unbroken for ages eternal, and is the Emperors' Throne of a truly single line. The Imperial Throne is the Throne of the Sovereign Lords who are the deific offspring of the Imperial Ancestor, who inherit the Land founded by the Imperial Ancestors, and make it their great august task to govern it peacefully as a peaceful Land,[7] and is the station of the Emperors who, one with the Imperial Ancestor, manifest their great august Will even until now, and who cause the Land to prosper and care for the people. The subjects, in looking up to the Emperor, who is deity incarnate, reverence at the same time the Imperial Ancestors, and under his bounty become the subjects of our country. Thus, the Imperial Throne is a Throne of the utmost dignity and is the foundation of a Land eternally firm.

That the Emperor who accedes to the Throne is descended from an unbroken line of sovereigns is the basis of the founding of the Land. [. . .] Namely, that the offspring of Amaterasu Ōmikami accede to the Throne from generation to generation is a great law which is forever unalterable. It indeed seems inevitable that in foreign countries, where conglomerations of individuals form a nation, rulers, on a basis of intelligence, virtues, and power, accede to a position because of their virtues, [. . .] or that they rise to positions of governors through power, and [it seems inevitable, too] that they are, through loss of power, deprived of their position, or also that they, completely subject to the people who exercise power, are chosen by election, etc.,

---

6. The Kojiki *and the* Nihon-shoki, *both written in the eighth century, are the oldest known histories of Japan.*

7. Yasu-kuni, *from which comes the name of one of Japan's most important shrines, which honors the spirits of fallen soldiers and sailors.*

and that decisions regarding them are purely the result of men's doings and men's influences. Moreover, as for these virtues and power, they are correlative, so that of necessity conflicts arise through the influence of power and personal interests, and this naturally makes a nation subject to revolutions. In our country, however, the Imperial Throne is acceded to by one descended from a line of Emperors unbroken for ages eternal, and is absolutely firm. Consequently, the Emperor, who sits upon such an Imperial Throne, is naturally endowed with gracious virtues, so that the Throne is so much the firmer and is also sacred. That the subjects should serve the Emperor is not because of duty as such, nor is it submission to authority; but is the natural manifestation of the heart and is the spontaneous obedience of deep faith toward His Majesty. We subjects hold in awe the cause behind the prosperity of the Imperial Line and its dignity, of which there is no parallel in foreign countries. [. . .]

II. The Sacred Virtues

Love for the People

Evidences of the Emperor's endless love and care for his subjects are constantly seen throughout history. The Emperor graciously treats his subjects as *ōmitakara*,[8] loves and protects them as one would sucklings, and, depending upon their cooperation, diffuses his policies widely. With this great august Will the successive Emperors directed their august minds towards the happiness of their subjects, not merely encouraging them to do what is right but pitying and putting aright those who had gone astray. [. . .]

The Emperor does not look upon his subjects as just his own, but as descendants of the subjects of the Imperial Ancestors. In the Imperial Rescript issued on the occasion of the promulgation of the Constitution, the Emperor Meiji says: "We recall the fact that Our subjects are descendants of the Imperial Ancestors' good and faithful subjects."

III. The Way of the Subjects

The Subjects

Here the authors define the relationship between the emperor and his subjects. They distinguish this relationship from that which exists between rulers and ruled in Western countries. Although in such places subjects or citizens may offer support to their sovereigns, they do not possess the bond that exists between them in Japan.

We have already witnessed the boundless Imperial virtues. Wherever this Imperial virtue of compassion radiates, the Way for the subjects naturally becomes clear. The Way of the subjects exists where the entire nation serves the Emperor

---

8. *Great treasures.*

united in mind in the very spirit in which many deities served at the time when the Imperial Grandchild, Ninigi no Mikoto, descended to earth. That is, we from birth serve the Emperor and walk the Way of the Empire, and it is perfectly natural that we subjects should possess this essential quality.

We subjects are intrinsically quite different from the so-called citizens of Occidental countries. The relationship between ruler and subject is not of a kind in which the people are correlated to the sovereign or in which there is first a people for whose prosperity and well-being a ruler is established. But the reason for erring as to the essential qualities of these subjects, or for looking upon them as being the same as so-called citizens [. . .] is that a clear-cut view concerning the cardinal principles of our national entity is lacking and confusion arises as a result of an ambiguous understanding of foreign theories about States. When citizens who are conglomerations of separate individuals independent of each other give support to a ruler in correlation to the ruler, there exists no deep foundation between ruler and citizen to unite them. However, the relationship between the Emperor and his subjects arises from the same fountainhead, and has prospered ever since the founding of the nation as one in essence. This is our nation's great Way and consequently forms the source of the Way of our subjects, and there is a radical difference between [ours] and foreign countries in the matter of choice. Needless to say, even in foreign countries their respective histories, as between ruler and citizens, differ, and there are bonds that attend these relationships. Nevertheless, a country such as ours which, since its founding, has seen a Way naturally one in essence with nature and man united as one, and which thereby has prospered all the more, cannot find its counterpart among foreign countries. Herein lies our national entity which is unparalleled in the world, and the Way of our subjects has its reason for being simply on the basis of this national entity, and on this, too, are based loyalty and filial piety.

Loyalty and Patriotism

Our country is established with the Emperor, who is a descendant of Amaterasu Ōmikami, as her center, and our ancestors as well as we ourselves constantly behold in the Emperor the fountainhead of her life and activities. For this reason, to serve the Emperor and to receive the Emperor's great august Will as one's own is the rationale of making our historical "life" live in the present; and on this is based the morality of the people.

Loyalty means to reverence the Emperor as [our] pivot and to follow him implicitly. By implicit obedience is meant casting ourselves aside and serving the Emperor intently. To walk this Way of loyalty is the sole Way in which we subjects may "live," and the fountainhead of all energy. Hence, offering our lives for the sake of the Emperor does not mean so-called self-sacrifice, but the casting aside of our little selves to live under his august grace and the enhancing of the genuine life of the people of a State. The relationship between the Emperor and the subjects is not an artificial relationship [which means] bowing down to authority, nor a relationship such as [exists] between master and servant as is seen in feudal morals. [. . .] The ideology which interprets the relationship between the Emperor and his subjects as being a reciprocal relationship such as merely [involves] obedience to authority or rights and duties, rests on individualistic ideologies, and is a rationalistic way of thinking that looks on everything as being in equal personal relationships. An individual is an existence belonging to a State and her history which form the basis of his origin, and is fundamentally one body with it. However, even if one were to think of a nation contrariwise and also to set up a morality by separating the individual alone from this one body, with this separated individual as the basis, one would only end in a so-called abstract argument that has lost its basis.

[. . .] The Imperial Ancestor and the Emperor are in the relationship of parent and child, and, the relationship between the Emperor and his subjects is, in its righteousness, that of sovereign and subject and, in its sympathies, that of father and child. This relationship is an "essential"[9] relationship that is far more fundamental than the rational, obligatory relationships, and herein are the grounds that give birth to the Way of loyalty. From the point of individualistic personal relationships, the relationship between sovereign and subject in our country may [perhaps] be looked upon as that between non-personalities. However, this is nothing but an error arising from treating the individual as supreme, from the notion that has individual thoughts for its nucleus, and from personal abstract consciousness. Our relationship between sovereign and subject is by no means a shallow, lateral relationship such as [means] the correlation between ruler and citizen, but is a relationship springing from a basis transcending this correlation, and is that of self-effacement and a return to [the] "one,"[1] in which this basis is not lost. This is a thing that can never be understood from an individualistic way of thinking. In our country, this great Way has seen a natural development since the founding of the nation, and the most basic thing that has manifested itself as regards the subjects is in short this Way of loyalty. Herein exists the profound meaning and lofty value of loyalty. Of late years, through the influence of the Occidental individualistic ideology, a way of thinking which has for its basis the individual has become lively. [. . .] [T]hose in our country who at the present time expound loyalty and patriotism are apt to lose [sight of] its true significance, being influenced by Occidental individualism and rationalism. We must sweep aside the corruption of the spirit and the clouding of knowledge that arises from setting up one's "self" and from being taken up with one's "self" and return to a pure and clear state of mind that belongs intrinsically to us as subjects, and thereby fathom the great principle of loyalty.

The Emperor always honors the Imperial Ancestors, and, taking the lead of his subjects, shows by practice the oneness of ancestor and offspring, and sets an

---

9. *That is, having to do with natural qualities.*

1. *That is, the casting away of self and returning to the "great Way."*

example of reverence for the deities and for the ancestors. Again, we subjects, as descendants of subjects who served the Imperial Ancestors, revere their ancestors, inherit their motives of loyalty, make this [spirit] "live" in the present, and pass it on to posterity. Thus, reverence for the deities and for the ancestors and the Way of loyalty are basically entirely one, and are Ways essentially inseparable. Such unity is seen in our country alone, and here, too, is the reason why our national entity is sacred.

The perfect unity between reverence for the deities and the Way of loyalty is also accounted for by the fact that these things and patriotism are one. To begin with, our country is one great family nation [comprising] a union of sovereign and subject, having the Imperial Household as the head family, and looking up to the Emperor as the focal point from of old to the present. Accordingly, to contribute to the prosperity of the nation is to serve for the prosperity of the Emperor; and to be loyal to the Emperor means nothing short of loving the country and striving for the welfare of the nation. Without loyalty there is no patriotism, and without patriotism there is no loyalty. All patriotism is always impregnated with the highest sentiments of loyalty, and all loyalty is always attended with the zeal of patriotism. Of course, in foreign countries, too, there exists a spirit of patriotism. But this patriotism is not of a kind which, like in our country, is from the very roots one with loyalty and in perfect accord with reverence for the deities and the ancestors.

Indeed, loyalty is our fundamental Way as subjects, and is the basis of our national morality. Through loyalty are we become Japanese subjects; in loyalty do we obtain life; and herein do we find the source of all morality. According to our history, the spirit of loyalty always runs through the hearts of the people. [. . .]

Loyalty is realized through the people's constant attention to duties and through faithful devotion to their pursuits. As graciously manifested in the Imperial Rescript on Education: not only to offer oneself courageously to the State, should occasion arise; but also to be filial to one's parents, affectionate to one's brothers and sisters, to be harmonious as husbands and wives, to be true as friends, to bear oneself in modesty and moderation, to extend one's benevolence to all, to pursue learning and to cultivate arts, and thereby to develop intellectual faculties and to perfect moral powers; furthermore, to advance public good and to promote common interests, always to respect the Constitution and to observe the laws, etc., are one and all accounted for by our response to the great august Will and our respectful support for His Majesty's diffusion of His enterprises, and all constitute the Way of loyalty. [. . .]

Verily, for those engaged in government, those engaged in industries, those that have dedicated themselves to education or scholastic pursuits, for them to devote themselves to their various fields, is the Way of loyalty to sustain the prosperity of the Imperial Throne, and is by no means a personal Way. [. . .]

Filial Piety

The authors take care to distinguish the Japanese manner of filial piety from that of China. Since the Chinese notion does not extend to the ruler—in other words, since there is nothing equivalent to the Japanese emperor in China—it is an inferior sort of filial piety. This is a prime example of how Japan has "sublimated" a foreign idea (that is, Chinese Confucianism) into its national entity, and in the process improved both.

In our country filial piety is a Way of the highest importance. Filial piety originates with one's family as its basis, and in its larger sense has the nation for its foundation. Filial piety directly has for its object one's parents, but in its relationship toward the Emperor finds a place within loyalty. [. . .]

The relationship between parent and child is a natural one, and therein springs the affection between parent and child. Parent and child are a continuation of one chain of life; and since parents are the source of the children, there spontaneously arises toward the children a tender feeling to foster them. Since children are expansions of parents, there springs a sense of respect, love for, and indebtedness toward, parents. [. . .]

Loyalty and Filial Piety as One

Filial piety in our country has its true characteristics in its perfect conformity with our national entity by heightening still further the relationship between morality and nature. Our country is a great family nation, and the Imperial Household is the head family of the subjects and the nucleus of national life. The subjects revere the Imperial Household, which is the head family, with the tender esteem [they have] for their ancestors; and the Emperor loves his subjects as his very own. [. . .]

Since our ancestors rendered assistance to the spreading of Imperial enterprises by the successive Emperors, for us to show loyalty to the Emperor is in effect a manifestation of the manners and customs of our ancestors; and this is why we show filial piety to our forefathers. In our country there is no filial piety apart from loyalty, and filial piety has loyalty for its basis. The logic of the unity of loyalty and filial piety based on national entity herein shines forth beautifully. [. . .]

In China, too, importance is laid on filial duty, and they say that it is the source of a hundred deeds. In India, too, gratitude to parents is taught. But their filial piety is not of a kind related to or based on the nation. Filial piety is a characteristic of Oriental morals; and it is in its convergence with loyalty that we find a characteristic of our national morals, and this is a factor without parallel in the world. [. . .]

Thus, the hearts of the subjects that render service through the Way of loyalty and filial piety as one, in uniting with the Emperor's great august heart of benevolence, reap the fruits of concord between the Sovereign and his subjects, and is the basic power of our nation's endless development.

Verily, loyalty and filial piety as one is the flower of our national entity, and is the cardinal point of our people's morals. Hence, national entity forms not only the foundation of morality but of all branches of such things as politics, economics, and industry. Accordingly, the great Way of loyalty and filial piety as one must be made manifest in all practical fields of these national activities and the people's lives. We subjects must strive all the more in loyalty and filial piety for the real manifestation of the immense and endless national entity.

IV. Harmony and Truth

Harmony

Here the authors claim that there can be no "true harmony" in Western states, since their people are too individualistic, and their governments based on social contract theories. When problems arise in Japan, they come from certain individuals—probably acting under the influence of foreign ideas—who behave contrary to the spirit of harmony. Society on the whole, however, remains free of conflict. It follows, then, that the country will thrive to the extent that its people conform to the official orthodoxy.

When we trace the marks of the facts of the founding of our country and the progress of our history, what we always find there is the spirit of harmony. Harmony is a product of the great achievements of the founding of the nation, and is the power behind our historical growth; while it is also a humanitarian Way inseparable from our daily lives. The spirit of harmony is built on the concord of all creation. When people determinedly count themselves as masters and assert their egos, there is nothing but contradictions and the setting of one against the other; and harmony is not begotten. In individualism it is possible to have cooperation, compromise, sacrifice, etc., so as to regulate and mitigate this contradiction and the setting of one against the other; but after all there exists no true harmony. That is, the society of individualism is one of clashes between a people and a people,[2] and history may be all looked upon as that of class wars. Social structure and political systems in such a society, and the theories of sociology, political science, statecraft, etc., which are their logical manifestations, are essentially different from those of our country which makes harmony its fundamental Way. Herein indeed lies the reason why the ideologies of our nation are different from those of the nations of the West.

Harmony as of our nation is not a mechanical concert of independent individuals of the same level that has its starting point in reason, but a great harmony that holds itself together by having the parts within the whole through actions that fit the parts. Hence therein is practiced mutual respectful love and obedience, endearment and fostering. This is not a mere compromise or concord of mechanical or homogeneous things; but is [a thing]—with all things having their characteristics, mutually different and yet manifesting their characteristics, that is, manifesting the essential qualities through the parts—that thus harmonize with

---

2. *Literally, "ten thousand men versus ten thousand men."*

the monastic world. That is, harmony as in our nation is a great harmony of individuals who, by giving play to their characteristics, and through difficulties, toil and labor, converge into one. Because of characteristics and difficulties, this harmony becomes all the greater and its substance rich. Again, in this way individualities are developed, special characteristics become beautiful, and at the same time even enhance the development and well-being of the whole. Indeed, harmony in our nation is not a half-measure harmony, but a great, practical harmony that manifests itself with freshness in step with the development of all things.

The Martial Spirit

And then, this harmony is clearly seen also in our nation's martial spirit. Our nation is one that holds *bushido* in high regard, and there are shrines deifying warlike spirits. [. . .] But this martial spirit does not exist for the sake of itself but for the sake of peace, and is what may be called a sacred martial spirit. Our martial spirit does not have for its objective the killing of men, but the giving of life to men. This martial spirit is that which tries to give life to all things, and is not that which destroys. That is to say, it is a strife which has peace at its basis with a promise to raise and to develop; and it gives life to things through its strife. Here lies the martial spirit of our nation. War, in this sense, is not by any means intended for the destruction, overpowering, or subjugation of others; and it should be a thing for the bringing about of great harmony, that is, peace, doing the work of creation by following the Way.

Musubi *and Harmony*

Through such harmony as this are our national creations and developments materialized. *Musubi* is "creation," and it is in effect a manifestation of the power of harmony. [. . .] *Musubi* comes from *musu*. *Musu*, as in *koke musu* [moss grows], means the generating of things. When things harmonize there is *musubi*. Hence, through harmony and mutual fellowship between sovereign and subject is a nation created and developed. The various national reforms and improvements, too, which are a problem of the day, must follow this *musubi* which is brought about by harmony. This must mean the correcting of wrongs by examining oneself in the light of our national entity under the august grace of the Emperor and the lively bringing forth of new fruits through great harmony. [. . .]

Mutual Harmony among the People

This harmonious spirit is also widely realized in the life of the nation. In our country, under a unique family system, parent and child and husband and wife live together, supporting and helping each other. In the Imperial Rescript on Education the Emperor Meiji graciously says: "Husbands and wives, be harmonious." And this harmony between husband and wife must merge into and become one with: "Be filial to your parents." That is, a family must be a place where there prospers a well-merged, united harmony in the union of a vertical harmony between parents and children and of a lateral harmony among husbands and wives, brothers and sisters.

Going a step further, this harmony must also be made to materialize in communal life. Those serving in Government offices as well as those working in firms must follow this Way of harmony. In each community there are those who take the upper places while there are those who work below them. Through each one fulfilling his portion is the harmony of a community obtained. To fulfill one's part means to do one's appointed task with the utmost faithfulness each in his own sphere; and by this means do those above receive help from inferiors, and inferiors are loved by superiors; and in working together harmoniously is beautiful concord manifested and creative work carried out.

This applies both to the community and to the State. In order to bring national harmony to fruition, there is no way but for every person in the nation to do his allotted duty and to exalt it. Those in high positions, low positions, rich, and poor, in or out of official life, those holding public or private positions, as well as those engaged in agriculture, industries, trade, etc., should not stand aloof one from the other by being taken up with themselves, but should not fail to make harmony their foundation.

In short, in our country, differences of opinion or of interests that result from one's position easily [merge] into one through our unique great harmony which springs from the same source. In all things strife is not the final goal, but harmony; all things do not end with destruction, but bear fruit in their fulfillment. Herein is the great spirit of our nation. In this manner is every progress and development seen in our nation carried out. [. . .]

Sovereign and Subjects in One

Here the authors suggest that world peace can only come when Japan's "harmonious spirit" prevails in all nations.

In our country, Sovereign and subjects have from of old been spoken of as being one, and the entire nation, united in mind and acting in full cooperation, have shown forth the beauties of this oneness with the Emperor as their center. The august virtues of the Emperor and the duties of the subjects converge and unite into a beautiful harmony. [. . .]

It is when this harmonious spirit of our nation is spread abroad throughout the world and every race and State, with due attention to its appointed duties, gives full play to its own characteristics, that true world peace and its progress and prosperity are realized.

Truth

A true heart is the most genuine thing in the spirit of man. Man has his basis of life in truth, through truth he becomes one with all things, gives life to and harmonizes with all things. [. . .]

[. . .] That is to say, it is a genuine heart and a genuine deed that is freed of self. Indeed, truth melts and unites together all things, releasing them of encumbrances. Truth manifested in art becomes beauty, and as morality becomes goodness, and in knowledge, veracity. It is to be noted that truth exists in the source which gives birth to beauty, goodness, and veracity. Thus, truth is in turn what is generally spoken of as a bright, clean, honest heart, that is to say, *Seimeishin* [clear, bright heart], and this forms the basis of our national spirit.

Since truth is the fountainhead of reason, will, and emotion; knowledge, pity, and courage may be looked upon as manifestations of truth. Our national Way by no means counts it sufficient to have courage alone. To let courage alone run away with oneself means courage of a low quality, so that both courage and pity need go together. Hence, in order to manifest courage and pity there must needs be knowledge. That means, these three things meet as one truth, and through truth these three work together efficaciously. [. . .]

Furthermore, actions carried out with sincerity are indeed genuine actions. Genuine words, genuine actions. Words that can be turned into actions are indeed genuine words. Our national idea of words has its basis here; so that as for words that cannot be turned into action, one must be discreet and not utter them. This is the heart of man as it should be. Words full of truth are in effect words of the soul; and such words are inherent with great deeds, that is, have infinitely strong power, and speak with an endless breadth. [. . .] Once a thing is said, one must by all means put it into practice; so that one should not utter at random words that cannot be followed by actions. Accordingly, once a thing is started, it must by every means be practiced. Nay, if genuine words,[3] they must of necessity be put into practice. Thus, at the roots of words that can be turned into actions there is truth. There must be no self in truth. When one speaks and acts, utterly casting oneself aside, there indeed is truth, and there indeed shines truth.

BOOK II: THE MANIFESTATION OF OUR NATIONAL ENTITY IN HISTORY

III. The Inherent Character of the People

* * *

A Clean and Cloudless Heart

In this chapter and the following, the authors stress the importance of "dying to self"; in other words, offering oneself completely in devotion to the emperor. This does not represent a true sacrifice, but merely a surrender of one's ego to the interest of the collective whole. This spirit of "self-effacement" is what allows the Japanese to assimilate foreign ideas without surrendering what is authentically Japanese.

---

3. Literally, "words of the soul."

Such a homeland as this and the national life which centers round the family, and which is expressive of the concord between the sovereign and the people, have together brought forth our national character that is cloudless, pure, and honest. [. . .]

A pure, cloudless heart is a heart which, dying to one's ego and one's own ends, finds life in fundamentals and the true Way. That means, it is a heart that lives in the Way of unity between the Sovereign and his subjects, a Way that has come down to us ever since the founding of the Empire. It is herein that there springs up a frame of mind, unclouded and right, that bids farewell to unwholesome self-interest. The spirit that sacrifices self and seeks life at the very fountainhead of things manifests itself eventually as patriotism and as a heart that casts self aside in order to serve the State. On the contrary, a heart that is taken up with self and lays plans solely for self has been looked upon, from of old, as filthy and impure; so that efforts have been made to exorcise and to get rid of it. [. . .]

When man makes self the center of his interests, the spirit of self-effacement and self-sacrifice suffers loss. In the world of individualism there naturally arises a mind that makes self the master and others servants and puts gain first and gives service a secondary place. Such things as individualism and liberalism, which are fundamental concepts of the nations of the West on which their national characteristics and lives are built, find their real differences when compared with our national concepts. Our nation has, since its founding, developed on the basis of a pure, unclouded, and contrite heart; and our language, customs, and habits all emanate from this source.

Self-Effacement and Assimilation

In the inherent character of our people there is strongly manifested, alongside with this spirit of self-effacement and disinterestedness, a spirit of broadmindedness and its activities. In the importation of culture from the Asiatic Continent, too, in the process of "dying to self" and adopting the ideographs used in Chinese classics, this spirit of ours has coordinated and assimilated these same ideographs. To have brought forth a culture uniquely our own, in spite of the fact that a culture essentially different was imported, is due entirely to a mighty influence peculiar to our nation. This is a matter that must be taken into serious consideration in the adaptation of modern Occidental culture.

The spirit of self-effacement is not a mere denial of oneself, but means the living to the great, true self by denying one's small self. Individuals are essentially not beings isolated from the State, but each has his allotted share as forming parts of the State. And because they form parts, they constantly and intrinsically unite themselves with the State; and it is this that gives birth to the spirit of self-effacement. And at the same time, because they form parts, they lay importance on their own characteristics and through these characteristics render service to the State. These characteristics, in union with the spirit of self-effacement, give rise to a power to assimilate things alien to oneself. In speaking of self-effacement or self-sacrifice, one does not mean the denial of oneself toward the State, such as exists in foreign countries, where the State and individuals are viewed correlatively. Again, by broadmindedness and assimilation is not meant the robbery of things alien by depriving them of characteristics peculiar to them, thereby bringing about the loss of their individuality, but is meant the casting aside of their defects and making the best use of their merits; so that by searching widely one may enrich oneself. Herein do we find the great strength of our nation and the depth and breadth of our ideologies and civilization. [. . .]

IV. Ceremonial Rites and Morality

Ceremonial Rites

Our country is a divine country governed by an Emperor who is a deity incarnate. The Emperor becomes one in essence with the heavenly deities by offering them worship, and thereby makes all the more clear his virtue as a deity incarnate. Hence, the Emperor lays particular importance on ceremonial rites; and in the ceremonial rites held in the three shrines in the Imperial Palace, namely, the Imperial Sanctuary, the Imperial Ancestors' Shrine, and the Imperial Tabernacle, the Emperor conducts the services himself. [. . .]

It is the nature of the subjects to make this great august Will their own, to receive the spirit of the founding of the Empire as their own by means of ceremonial rites, to pray for the Emperor's peace by sacrificing themselves, and to enhance the spirit of service to the State. Thus, the Emperor's service to the deities and the subjects' reverence for the deities both spring from the name source; and the Emperor's virtues are heightened all the more by means of the ceremonial rites, and the subjects' determination to fulfill their duties is made all the more firm through their reverence for the deities.

Our shrines have served, from of old, as the center of the spirit of ceremonial rites and functions. Shrines are expressions of the great Way of the deities and places where one serves the deities and repays the source of all things and returns to their genesis. [. . .]

The deities enshrined in the Shinto shrines are the Imperial Ancestors, the ancestors of the clans descended from the heavenly deities or the Imperial Family, and the divine spirits who served to guard and maintain the prosperity of the Imperial Throne. These ceremonial rites of the Shinto shrines serve to foster the life of our people and form the basis of this spirit. In the festivals of the clan deities one sees expressions of the spirit of repaying the source of all things and of returning to their genesis, and of the consequent concourse of clansmen. Then again, in the festival rites of the guardian deities, in which portable shrines are borne along, there is the friendly gathering of parishioners and the peaceful scenes of the villages. Hence, Shinto shrines are also the center of the people's life in their home towns. Further, on national holidays the people put up the Rising Sun flag and unite in their national spirit of devotion to the State. Thus, all functions of the Shinto shrines ultimately unite in the services rendered by the Emperor to the Imperial Ancestors; and it is in this that we find the basis of our national reverence for the deities. [. . .]

The true purport of our nation's ceremonial rites has been expounded in the foregoing passages; and when this is compared with faith toward God as it exists in the Occident, the result is a great gap. In the mythologies and legends of the West, too, mention is made of many deities; but these are not national deities that have been linked with the nation since the days of their origin, nor are they deities that have given birth to the people or the Land or have brought them up. Reverence toward deities in our country is a national faith based on the spirit of the founding of the Empire, and is not a faith toward a transcendental God in the world of Heaven, Paradise, Paramita [Sanskrit], or the ideal, but it is a spirit of service that flows out naturally from the historical life of the people. Hence, our ceremonial rites have a deep and broad significance, and at the same time are truly national and allied to actual life.

Morality

It is this spirit of reverence for the deities and one's ancestors that forms the basis of our national morality; and it is also this that has embraced and assimilated Confucianism, Buddhism, and other things imported from abroad into every field of our culture and created things truly Japanese. Our national morality is founded on reverence for the deities and our ancestors, and has brought forth the fruits of the great principle of loyalty and filial piety. By making the nation our home, loyalty becomes filial piety; and by making our homes our nation, filial piety becomes loyalty. Herein do loyalty and filial piety join in one and become the source of all good.

Loyalty means engaging ourselves zealously in our duties by making it our fundamental principle to be candid, clean, and honest, and it means fulfilling our duties, and thus to serve the Emperor; and by making loyalty our basic principle is filial piety established. This is the great Way of the deities which our people have faithfully followed since the days of their ancestors and throughout the past and the present. [. . .]

BUSHIDO

This section is noteworthy for the authors' association of Bushido—*the ancient way of the warriors—with modern totalitarianism.*

Bushido may be cited as showing an outstanding characteristic [of] our national morality. In the world of warriors one sees inherited the totalitarian structure and spirit of the ancient clans peculiar to our nation. Hence, though the teachings of Confucianism and Buddhism have been followed, these have been transcended. That is to say, though a sense of obligation binds master and servant, this has developed into a spirit of self-effacement and of meeting death with a perfect calmness. In this, it was not that death was made light of so much as that man tempered himself to death, and in a true sense regarded it with esteem. In effect, man tried to fulfill true life by way of death. This means that rather than lose the whole by being taken up with and setting up oneself, one puts self to death in order to give full play to the whole by fulfilling the whole. Life and death are basically one, and the monistic truth is found where life and death are transcended. Through this is life, and through this is death. However, to treat life and death as two opposites and to hate death and to seek life is to be taken up with one's own interests, and is a thing of which warriors are ashamed. To fulfill the Way of loyalty, counting life and death as one, is *Bushido*. [. . .]

V. National Culture

Culture

> *The authors again extol the Japanese talent for assimilating and sublimating foreign ideas, accepting and improving those that are good and rejecting those that are destructive of the national entity.*

Our culture is a manifestation of the great spirit that has come down to us since the founding of the Empire. In order to enrich and develop this, foreign culture has been assimilated and sublimated. In the *Gozatsuso*, a product of the Ming Dynasty in China, there is a tradition [. . .] which says that if there should be anyone going over to Japan carrying with him the works of Mencius[4] his boat would be overturned and those on board be drowned. This goes to show that all revolutionary ideas are basically contrary to our national entity and proves the existence of our resolute spirit and our impartial judgment which is based thereon. [. . .]

No true culture should be the fruit of abstract individual ideas alienated from the State and the race. Every cultural feature in our country is an embodiment of our national entity. When one looks upon culture as developments of abstract ideas, the result is always separation from concrete history, and the inevitable is something abstract and universal that transcends national boundaries. However, in our culture there always subsists the spirit of the founding of the Empire, and this spirit is one in essence with our history.

Thus, our national culture is consistent in spirit and at the same time brings to view characteristics differing with every stage of history. Hence, creation always means union with retrospection, and restorations always become the generative power behind reformations. That means that the present and the past unite in one; and it is here that creative activities of a new era are carried on. [. . .]

---

4. *Mencius (379–281 B.C.E.) was a Chinese philosopher and legendary Confucian scholar. His political thought emphasizes the goodness of individuals and the duty of rulers to govern with their people's interests at heart. He goes so far as to suggest that people have a right to overthrow their ruler if he fails to do so, which helps explain why the authors have included this saying.*

Artistic Pursuits

Our national Way stands out markedly in the arts that have come down to us from of old. Poetry, music, calligraphy, painting, the incense cult, the tea ceremony, flower arrangement, architecture, sculpture, industrial arts, and dramas, all culminate in the Way, and find their source therein. The Way manifests itself on the one hand as a spirit of esteem for tradition and on the other as creative or progressive activities. Thus, our artistic pursuits, ever since the Middle Ages, have been practiced by first keeping to the norms, and by later laying emphasis on cultural methods of getting away from these norms. This means that they taught that artistic pursuits should be materialized along one's personality only after one has personally found the Way by casting aside one's untoward desires and by first following the norms in keeping with tradition. This is characteristic of our artistic pursuits and training therein. [. . .]

In a word, our culture is in its essence a manifestation of the great spirit of the founding of the Empire; and scholastic pursuits, education, artistic pursuits, etc., all spring from one and the same source. Our future national culture, too, must be increasingly evolved in keeping with a Way such as this.

VI. Political, Economic, and Military Affairs

* * *

Constitution Granted by the Emperor

In this section and the next, the authors explain that Japan's written constitution is fundamentally different from those of other countries. Rather than emerging out of a struggle between ruler and ruled or among interest groups, it was announced as "an Imperial edict." This means that, far from being based on a social contract or a means of limiting the emperor's authority, it reaffirms his absolute authority. Further, it means that the movements toward constitutionalism and parliamentary government that had been developing since the 1890s were wholly illegitimate. Nor do individuals possess inherent rights under the constitution, as this would run counter to the Japanese notion of "dying to self" in service to the emperor.

The Emperor Meiji, transmitting the teachings bequeathed by the Imperial Ancestors and the great law marking the reigns of the successive Emperors, graciously enacted the Imperial House Law on February 11, 1889, and promulgated the Constitution of the Japanese Empire.

The written Constitutions of foreign countries have come into existence as a result, in the main, of expelling or suppressing the existing ruler. In the case of a Constitution resulting from the expulsion of a ruler, the thing is called a Constitution based on Social Contract; but in reality it is not a thing contracted by a people on an equal level and on a free footing, but is nothing short of a thing settled upon by winners in a struggle for power. A Constitution resulting through the suppression of a ruler is referred to as a Constitution contracted between Ruler and People; and this is nothing but a matter agreed upon between a ruler traditionally in power and a rising influence which coerces him to enter into an agreement touching their respective spheres of influence. [. . .]

However, our Imperial Constitution is a Constitution granted by the Throne, which the Emperor who comes of a line unbroken for ages eternal has instituted in perfect accord with his great august Will by virtue of the "supreme authority bestowed upon him by the Imperial Ancestors"; so that, together with the Imperial House Law, it is indeed nothing short of an Imperial edict.

Hence, the substance of this Constitution granted by the Throne is not a thing that has been turned into a norm, in order to stabilize forever, as in foreign countries, the authoritative factors to the time of the enactment of a Constitution. Nor is it the fruit of a systematization or abstract ideas or practical requirements of such things as democracy, government by the law, constitutionalism, communism, or dictatorship. Nor again is it an imitation or adaptation of a foreign system, but it is nothing less than the great law of administration clearly manifested in the injunctions bequeathed by the Imperial Ancestors. [. . .]

When we note the august spirit to establish a Constitution, such as referred to, and turn our attention to the origins of the enactment of Constitutions among foreign nations, we can understand the essential differences between our Constitution and those of foreign nations. [. . .]

Direct Rule by the Emperor

Furthermore, the other provisions of the Imperial Constitution are standing rules for government by the Emperor, who possesses all these essential qualities. Above all, the basic principles underlying the form of government are not [. . .] those of the British type of government in which "the sovereign reigns but does not rule"; nor yet are they the principles underlying joint government by a sovereign and his subjects; no more are they those underlying the policy of mutual independence of the legislature or the policy of binding everything under the law; but are entirely the basic principles of direct rule by the Emperor. [. . .]

All the laws in the Imperial Constitution on form of government are but extensions and transmissions of this principle of direct Imperial rule. For instance, stipulations on the rights and duties of Sovereign and subject are different from those which exist among Western nations, where a system of free rights serves to protect the inherent rights of the people from the ruler, for the stipulations are the fruit of the Emperor's fond care for his people and his great august spirit to provide them with equal opportunities for assisting the Throne without feelings of barrier. The triune subsistence, for example, of the Government, courts of justice, and the Diet, is different from the mutual independence of the legislature as it exists among Western nations, which aims at depriving the one holding sovereign power of judicial and legislative powers, giving recognition only to, yet at the same time curbing, his administrative power, with a view to restraining the powers of the ruler; for in our country segregation is not in respect of the rights of a ruler, but applies merely to the organs for the assistance of the direct Imperial rule, whose object is to make ever more secure the assistance extended to the direct rule by the Emperor. The deliberative assembly, too, is, in a so-called democratic country, a representative organ of a people who are nominal rulers; while in a so-called monarchy, where the sovereign and the people govern the nation together, the assembly is a representative organ of the people whose object is to hold the caprices of the sovereign under restraint and to provide a means by which the ruler and the people may govern the nation together. Our Imperial Diet, on the other hand, is completely different, since it was instituted with the one object of providing the people with a means of assisting the Emperor's direct rule in special ways in regard to special matters.

Our National Laws

Our national laws are one and all based on the Imperial House Law and the Imperial Constitution. Some of our statutes, laws, and regulations are established by direct Imperial sanction, while there are others that are established through the Emperor's authorization. There is, however, there is not one of all these statutes, laws, and regulations that does not find its source in His Majesty's august virtue. [. . .] As a consequence, our national laws are one and all expressions of our national entity.

Thus, our national laws are signposts to show the way by which the subjects may individually guard and maintain the prosperity of the Imperial Throne under His Majesty's august virtue, doing one's very best and so following His Majesty with awe. Hence, the basic reason for the subjects' respect for the Constitution and their observance of the national laws lies in their being true, loyal, and good subjects.

Economy

> The authors here warn against the dangers of Western political economy, particularly the classical liberal notion (exemplified by Adam Smith) that the public good can be served through individuals pursuing their own self-interest. While it is worthwhile to adapt the West's industrial methods, the pursuit of economic activities purely for personal gain goes against the Japanese way.

Economy is the essence of a nation's material life; and commodities are necessary not only for the preservation of a people's natural life but are an indispensable factor in enhancing the Imperial prestige. Hence, it follows that the promotion of the nation's economic strength forms a vital basis for the development of our Empire.

Consequently, in the very beginning of the founding of the Empire, our Imperial Ancestor graciously introduced trades, and taught that economy, namely, industries, comprised one of the great national enterprises. [. . .]

Our national economy is a great enterprise based on His Majesty's great august Will to have the Empire go on developing forever and ever, and is a thing on which the subjects' happiness depends; so that it is not a disconnected series of activities aimed at fulfilling the material desires of individual persons, a doctrine expounded by Western economists. It is a thing in which the entire nation joins the Way of *musubi*, each person fulfilling his duties according to the part he has been assigned to play. Agriculture, which developed early in our country, has meant the raising of crops through human efforts and the harmonious pursuit in the raising of crops between man and soil. This is the fundamental spirit of our national industries. Needless to say, commercial and industrial activities, though new to us, are things that must be engaged in with the same spirit.

It should be conceived that at the very basis of our modern economic activities there constantly runs this attitude toward industries that has come down to us since the founding of the Empire, in spite of the tremendous infiltration of Western ideas. This does not mean that every person in our country has always been awake to this spirit in his economic activities; nor does it mean that in all their industrial activities our people have been always free of harboring ideas of profit. But it cannot be overlooked that the majority of those engaged in our national industries have harmoniously occupied themselves in their work in a spirit to do their respective duties faithfully and well rather than to be led merely by the idea of fulfilling their own personal material desires. It is for this very reason that a leap forward that vies with the world, as we have seen of late, has been made in our industrial society.

The attitude of mind which is based on the spirit of *musubi*, and puts public interests before private ones, paying full attention to one's allotted duties and to being in harmony with others, has been an attitude toward industrial enterprises inherent in our nation; and it is a basic reason for the rise of a strong impetus in the world of industry, for encouraging initiative, stimulating cooperation, greatly heightening industrial efficiency, bringing about the prosperity of all industries, and for contributing toward the increase of national wealth. In our economic activities, we must in the future become fully awake to this particular attitude of mind toward industries, and with this consciousness strive more than ever to develop them. In this manner will economy conform with morals, and develop industries that are based on the Way and not on material profit, and be able to enhance the glory of our national entity in our economy.

Military Affairs

Here is outlined the duties of members of the armed forces; each soldier and sailor is obliged to carry out his assigned duties as if they were the express will of the Emperor.

The manifestation of our national entity is just the same also in the case of our military affairs. Since ancient times the spirits of the deities in our country have fallen into two groups: the spirits of peace and the spirits of warriors. Where there is a harmonious working of the two, all things under the sun rest in peace, grow, and develop. Hence, the warrior spirits work inseparably and as one with the spirits of peace. It is in the subduing of those who refuse to conform to the august influence of the Emperor's virtues that the mission of our Imperial Military Forces lies; and thus we see the Way of the warriors that may be called Jimmu.[5] [. . .]

Truly, the mission of the Imperial Forces lies in doing the Emperor's Will, in guarding the Empire in perfect conformity with his great august wishes, and in thus exalting the national prestige. Our Imperial Forces have come to hold a position of responsibility in which their duty is to make our national prestige greatly felt within and without our country, to preserve the peace of the Orient in the face of the world powers, and to preserve and enhance the happiness of mankind, now that our Forces, in this spirit, have gone through the experiences of the SinoJapanese and RussoJapanese Wars and have joined the World War.[6]

Thus, we must observe His Majesty's commands to the effect that our people should "follow their allotted duties both in the literary and military spheres, the masses bending their whole strength to their individual tasks"; and so must we discharge our duties as subjects by guarding and maintaining the prosperity of the Imperial Throne which is coeval with heaven and earth, cooperating as one and rendering wholehearted service to the Throne.

CONCLUSION

The authors now return to a central theme of the book—that the disharmony that has existed in Japan in recent years is the result of the failure of the Japanese people to sublimate Western ideas in the same way that they did Chinese ideas earlier in their history.

We have inquired into the fundamental principles of our national entity and the ways in which it has been manifested in our national history. What kind of resolve and attitude should we subjects of the Japanese Empire now take toward the various problems of the day? It seems to us that our first duty is the task of creating a new Japanese culture by sublimating and assimilating foreign cultures which are at the source of the various problems in keeping with the fundamental principles of our national entity.

Every type of foreign ideology that has been imported into our country may have been quite natural in China, India, Europe, or America, in that it has sprung from their racial or historical characteristics; but in our country, which has a unique national entity, it is necessary as a preliminary step to put these types to

---

5. *This is a play on words, since Jimmu, the name of the first emperor, literally means "divine warrior."*
6. *That is, World War I.*

rigid judgment and scrutiny so as to see if they are suitable to our national traits. That is to say, the creation of a new culture which has characteristics peculiar to our nation can be welcomed only through this consciousness and the sublimation and assimilation of foreign cultures that accompanies it.

Characteristics of Occidental Ideologies

The authors trace Western ideas to the Ancient Greeks, who valued rationalism and objectivity. They developed philosophy that was based purely on reason and hence believed their ideas were of universal validity. These ideas were then accepted by the Romans and then strengthened by Christianity, a dangerous religion in that it insisted that rulers were subject to God's laws. All the problems of contemporary Western society, the authors believe, stem from these faulty principles.

Occidental ideologies spring from Greek ideologies. Greek concepts, whose keynote is the intellectual spirit, are characterized by being rational, objective, and idealistic. Culture was shaped centering on cities, leaving to posterity philosophies and works of art rarely to be seen in human history; but toward the end of their days, individualistic tendencies gradually appeared in their ideologies and modes of life. Rome adapted and developed these Greek concepts in their laws, statecraft, and other practical fields, and at the same time adopted Christianity, which transcends the State. Modern concepts prevailing among European nations have arisen, on the one hand, with the aim of bringing about the Kingdom of Heaven on earth by reviving Greek ideologies and by claiming the liberation of individuals and the acquisition of their freedom in opposition to the religious oppressions and feudalistic despotism of the Middle Ages. On the other hand, their origin is seen in the attempt to put them into practice by carrying over the concepts that hold in high regard the qualities of universality and veracity that transcend the State as they existed in the Middle Ages. Hence, the astounding development of modern civilization that characterizes the history of the world, by bringing about the development of natural science—a civilization founded in the main on individualism, liberalism, and rationalism, in all the branches of education, scholastic pursuits, politics, and economics.

Human beings are real existences as well as historical existences linked with eternity. They are, furthermore, egos, as well as correlated existences. That is to say, their existences are ordained by a national spirit based on history. This is the basic character of human existence. Its real worth is found where this concrete existence as a people is kept in view, and people exist as individuals in that very state. However, the individualistic explanation of human beings abstracts only one aspect of an individuality and overlooks the national and historical qualities. Hence, it loses sight of the totality and concreteness of human beings and deviates from the reality of human existence, the theories departing from actualities and running off into many mistaken channels. Herein lie the basic errors underlying the various concepts of individualism, liberalism, and their developments. The nations of the West have now awakened to these errors, and various ideologies and movements have sprung up in order to overcome them. Nevertheless, these ideologies and movements will eventually end in regarding collections of people as bodies or classes, or at the most in conceiving a conceptual State; so that such things will do no more than provide erroneous ideas to take the place of existing erroneous ideas, and will furnish no true way out or solution.

Characteristics of Oriental Ideologies

The authors criticize Chinese Confucianism for having separated itself from political matters, and thereby becoming "individualistic."

Chinese ideologies introduced into our country were chiefly Confucianism and the philosophies of Laôtzŭ and Chuangtzŭ.[7] Confucianism excels in its matter as a practical doctrine and is invaluable as a teaching. Consequently, it has filial piety for its basis of teaching, and this is owing to the fact that in China moral doctrines are founded with the family as the center. This filial piety has practicable qualities, but is not perfected as in our country as a national system of morals in which there is a merging of loyalty and filial piety. China bases her national morals on family morals, as is seen in the saying that loyal subjects come from families where filial piety is practiced; but because of revolutions which involve change of dynasties and transference of the throne, her loyalty and filial piety cannot become the morality of a historical, concrete, eternal State. Laôtzŭ and Chuangtzŭ left this turbid world behind them and returned to nature, and harbored as their ideal an unsophisticated attitude of mind; which in the long run turned their doctrines into abstract notions that denied culture, so that they fell into individualism, not having stood on concrete and historical foundations. The followers of Laôtzŭ showed an inclination to live in seclusion, away from the world, like the Seven Wise Men of the Bamboo Grove[8], and became disciples of a lofty hermit life. In a word, we may say that in that these thoughts are lacking in concrete, national foundations that develop historically, the philosophies of Confucius, Laôtzŭ, and Chuangtzŭ, tend to become individualistic. But when adopted by our country, these philosophies shed themselves of their individualistic and revolutionary elements; so that Confucianism in particular was sublimated and assimilated into our national entity, bringing about the establishment of a Japanese Confucianism, and contributing greatly toward the development of our national morality. [. . .]

Creation of New Japanese Culture

To put it in a nutshell, while the strong points of Occidental learning and concepts lie in their analytical and intellectual qualities, the characteristics of Oriental

---

7. *In other words, the philosophy of Taoism.*

8. *A Western version of this might be the so-called ivory tower of academia.*

learning and concepts lie in their intuitive and ascetic qualities. These are natural tendencies that arise through racial and historical differences; and when we compare them with our national spirit, concepts, or mode of living, we cannot help recognizing further great and fundamental differences. Our nation has in the past imported, assimilated, and sublimated Chinese and Indian ideologies, and has therewith supported the Imperial Way, making possible the establishment of an original culture based on her national entity. Following the Meiji Restoration, Occidental cultures rushed in, and contributed immensely toward our national prosperity; but their individualistic qualities brought about various difficulties in all the phases of the lives of our people, causing their thoughts to fluctuate. However, now is the time for us to sublimate and assimilate these Occidental ideologies in keeping with our national entity, to set up a vast new Japanese culture, and, by taking advantage of these things, to bring about a great national development.

In introducing, sublimating, and assimilating Occidental cultures, it is necessary at the outset to inquire into the essence of Occidental institutions and ideologies. If this were not done, elucidation of the nature of our national entity might fall into abstractions that have lost sight of realities. Notable characteristics that mark modern Western cultures are the spectacular developments of the natural sciences, which are based on positivism and of the material civilization which is their fruit. Further, in the fields of mental sciences, too, there is the same precision and logical systematization and the shaping of unique cultures. Our nation must increasingly adopt these various sciences, and look forward to the advancement of our culture and national development. However, these scholastic systems, methods, and techniques are substantiated by views of life and of the world peculiar to the West, which views are due to the racial, historical, and topographical characteristics of the Occident. Hence, in introducing these things into our country, we must pay thorough attention to these points, scrutinize their essential qualities, and with the clearest insight adapt their merits and cast aside their demerits.

Various Reforms

The authors believe that the West is doomed because of its philosophy, but they are optimistic about Japan's future, because the national entity remains strong. The challenge is to distinguish those elements of foreign belief that are helpful from those that are destructive. The people need to be particularly on guard against individualism and rationalism, which are the underlying core of those ideas.

An examination of our national trends since the Meiji Restoration shows that there are those who, casting aside the traditional spirit, have immersed themselves in Western ideas; and those who, while holding to their historical faith, have fallen prey to dualistic concepts by accepting the scholastic theories of the West at face value, without giving them sufficient scrutiny. And what is more, there are those who have done this without being conscious of the fact. Again, the result has been a considerable intellectual gap between the intelligentsia, who have markedly come under the influence of Occidental ideologies, and the common people. Thus, such a situation has given rise to various knotty problems. The fact that such things as communist movements, which at one time were popular, or the recent question of the organ theory[9] in regard to the Emperor, have from time to time been taken up by a group of scholars and some of the intelligentsia, is an eloquent proof of the situation. Although communism of late appears to have fallen into decay and the organ theory to have been exploded, these things have by no means been thoroughly solved. So long as further progress is not made in the investigation of the true nature of Western ideologies in all fields, and their sublimation and assimilation by means of our national entity remains unrealized, it may be difficult to reap genuine results.

Everyone seems to realize that extreme Occidental ideologies and studies in general, such as communism and anarchism, fall wide of our national entity; but little attention is paid as to whether those ideologies and studies that are not extreme, such as democracy and liberalism, really accord with our national entity or not. Now, when we consider how modern Occidental ideologies have given birth to democracy, socialism, communism, anarchism, etc., we note, as already stated, the existence of historical backgrounds that form the bases of all these concepts, and, besides, the existence of individualistic views of life that lie at their very roots. The basic characteristics of modern Occidental cultures lie in the fact that an individual is looked upon as an [. . .] absolutely independent being, all cultures comprising the perfection of this individual being, who in turn is the creator and determiner of all values. Hence, value is laid on the subjective thoughts of an individual; the conception of a State, the planning of all systems, and the constructing of theories being solely based on ideas conceived in the individual's mind. The greater part of Occidental theories of State and political concepts so evolved do not view the State as being an organic entity that gives birth to individual beings, which it transcends, but as an expedient for the benefit, protection, and enhancement of the welfare of individual persons; so that these theories have become expressions of the principles of subsistence which have at their center free, equal, and independent individuals. As a result, there have arisen types of mistaken liberalism and democracy that have solely sought untrammeled freedom and forgotten moral freedom, which is service. Hence, wherever this individualism and its accompanying abstract concepts have developed, concrete and historical national life became

---

9. The "organ theory," advanced by Tokyo Imperial University legal scholar Minobe Tatsukichi in the late 1920s, held that in the Japanese government it was the kokutai itself that was supreme, and the emperor was merely an "organ" of that larger body. Traditionalists took strong exception to the organ theory, regarding it as an insult to the emperor and an attempt to shoehorn Japanese tradition into Western political theory. Minobe was ultimately forced to resign his faculty position, and certain of his works were banned.

lost in the shadow of abstract theories; all States and peoples were looked upon alike as nations in general and as individuals in general; such things as an international community comprising the entire world and universal theories common to the entire world were given importance, rather than concrete nations and their characteristic qualities; so that in the end there even arose the mistaken idea that international law constituted a higher norm than national laws, that it stood higher in value, and that national laws were, if anything, subordinate to it.

The beginnings of modern Western free economy are seen in the expectation to bring about national prosperity as a result of free, individual, lucrative activities. In the case of the introduction into our country of modern industrial organizations that had developed in the West, so long as the spirit to bring about national profit and the people's welfare governed the people's minds, the lively and free individual activities went very far toward contributing to the nation's wealth; but later, with the dissemination of individualistic and liberal ideas, there gradually arose a tendency openly to justify egoism in economic managements and operations. This tendency gave rise to the problem of a chasm between rich and poor, and finally became the cause of the rise of ideas of class warfare; while later the introduction of communism brought about the erroneous idea which looked upon economy as being the basis of politics, morality, and all other cultures, and which considered that by means of class warfare alone could an ideal society be realized. The fact that egoism and class warfare are opposed to our national entity needs no explanation. Only where the people, one and all, put heart and soul into their respective occupations, and there is coherence or order in everyone's activity, with their minds set on guarding and maintaining the prosperity of the Imperial Throne, is it possible to see a healthy development in the people's economic life. [. . .]

Thus, modern Occidental ideologies that have infiltrated all fields of education, scholastic pursuits, politics, and economics, amount to nothing short of individualism. Hence, it must be acknowledged that individualistic cultures have achieved the awakening of individuals to a sense of their individual values and stimulated the elevation of individual faculties. Nevertheless, as developments in the West show, individualism virtually provokes the setting up of an individual against an individual and classes against classes, and foments many problems and disturbances in the national and social life. In the Occident, too, many movements are now being carried out to revise individualism. Socialism and communism, which are types of class individualism, and which are the opposites of so-called bourgeois individualism, belong to these movements, while recent ideological movements, such as that known as Fascism, which are types of nationalism and racial consciousness, belong to this category.

In order, however, to correct the faults brought about by individualism in our country and to see a way out of the deadlock which it has created, it would be utterly impossible to do this, if we adopted such ideas as Occidental socialism and their abstract totalitarianism wholesale, or copied their concepts and plans, or else mechanically excluded Occidental cultures.

Our Mission

Our present mission as a people is to build up a new Japanese culture by adopting and sublimating Western cultures with our national entity as the basis, and to contribute spontaneously to the advancement of world culture. Our nation early saw the introduction of Chinese and Indian cultures, and even succeeded in evolving original creations and developments. This was made possible, indeed, by the profound and boundless nature of our national entity; so that the mission of the people to whom it is bequeathed is truly great in its historical significance. The call for a clarification of our national entity is at this time very much in the fore; but this must unfailingly be done by making the sublimation of Occidental ideologies and cultures its occasion, since, without this, the clarification of our national entity is apt to fall into abstractions isolated from actualities. That is to say, the adoption and sublimation of Occidental ideologies and the clarification of our national entity are so related as to be inseparable.

The attitude of the Japanese in the past toward the cultures of the world has been independent and yet at the same time comprehensive. Our contributions to the world lie only in giving full play more than ever to our Way, which is that of the Japanese people. The people must more than ever create and develop a new Japan by virtue of their immutable national entity, which is the basis of the State, and by virtue of the Way of the Empire, which stands firm throughout the ages at Home and abroad, and thereby more than ever guard and maintain the prosperity of the Imperial Throne, which is coeval with heaven and earth. This, indeed, is our mission.

NAGAI RYŪTARŌ

From "The White Peril," 1913

Nagai Ryūtarō (1881–1944) was born into a samurai family in Kanazawa. As a young man he converted to Christianity and studied in England at Manchester College, Oxford. Upon his return he taught at Waseda University and edited a monthly magazine (Shin Nippon). A political liberal, Nagai championed universal suffrage, social welfare, labor unions, and even rights for women. At the same time, he was deeply resentful of the racist, anti-Asian attitudes he encountered among Westerners, which led him to become one of the earliest advocates of Pan-Asianism (although he never used the term). Many Europeans and Americans of the age spoke of a "Yellow Peril," claiming that the West was in mortal danger from the peoples of East Asia. This was sheer fiction, Nagai countered; the real threat was the "White Peril," and its victims were the non-white peoples of the world. The nations of East Asia, therefore, needed to unite in resistance to "white imperialism."

SOURCE: *Nagai Ryūtarō, "The White Peril," The Japan Magazine, 1913, pp. 39–42.*

When Buckle[1] wrote his history of Civilization the Crimean War was at its height, and the whole of Europe was being regaled by the press with pictures of blood and carnage. To solace the wounded sensibilities of the public Buckle contended that in modern times wars were necessary as the inevitable defence of civilized states against the aggression of half civilized or savage nations, but he congratulated his countrymen on the conviction that the time was now past when one civilized people could take up arms against another for the purpose of mere aggression.

Who could have thought that immediately after this, civilized France would have gone to war with Austria [in 1859]; and that the combined forces of Prussia and Austria would have invaded Denmark and calmly appropriated Sleiswick and Holstein [in 1864]? Not very long afterwards came the conflict between France and Germany [in 1870], two highly civilized white nations. Then we have such unedifying spectacles as the war between America and Spain [in 1898], and the seizure of the South African Republics by the British [in the Boer War, 1899–1902]. In addition to this most of the nations of Europe have been carrying on a system of appropriating the land of the more uncivilized races too weak for self defence. The extent of territory taken by the white races in this way during the nineteenth century totals nearly 10,000,000 square miles embracing a population about 135,000,000. And it will be seen that even within the comparatively short space of time since 1860 the white races have taken nearly 10,000,000 square miles of land and enforced their rule over many millions of the darker skinned races! [. . .]

In the face of all this we have been treated by the white races in recent years to tracts, treaties and newspaper articles galore on what they are pleased to call, "The Yellow Peril." Surely, in comparison with the white races, there is no indication of any peril of yellow aggression, at least. We do not mean to condemn aggression independently of circumstances; for there might be the duty of interfering for the sake of opening up the resources of a people and thus promoting their wealth and happiness. Mr. Leroy-Beaulieu[2] [1843–1916] says that the human

---

1. *Henry Thomas Buckle (1821–1862) was an English historian who aspired to write a fourteen-volume History of Civilization in England. Only the first two volumes were published—the first, to which Nagai refers, in 1857—before Buckle's death.*

2. *Pierre Paul Leroy-Beaulieu (1843–1916) was a French economist, holder of the chair of political economy in the Collège de France and co-president of the Société d'Économie Politique.*

race may be classified as 1. Civilized Christian peoples; 2. Civilized Non-Christian races; 3. Half-civilized people; 4. Savage tribes. The former, he holds, have the right and obligation to lead the latter two classes to civilization, just as parents have the right and the duty to educate their children. According to this theory it would be unjust to reproach any nation for intruding upon a barbarous race to impose upon it civilized conditions. But the difficulty is that most of such interferences do not appear to be for any benevolent purpose, the motive being, for the most part, simply aggressive. On the authority of their own historians we are forced to convict the Spanish invaders of South America as bent chiefly on rapine and plunder of a very murderous kind, the number of people killed in 50 years being estimated at upwards of 10,000,000. In Mexico alone the number killed is calculated at 4,000,000. This does not take into account the terrible decimation of territory, leaving destruction everywhere in the wake of murder. In some cases the native tribes were furnished with arms and set fighting with one another so as to bring about self-destruction. Is it not a fact that many tribes have been wiped out by the white races? Others have been driven out from their ancient habitations, as witness the Kaffirs in South Africa. These are all conspicuous facts that do not lie. If it be said that such things belong to a past age of civilization, we point out the conduct of the Belgians in the Congo, where under the plea of protection and development of territory, heavy taxes have been imposed on the miserable natives, and the refusal to comply with arbitrary exactions visited with the crudest of punishments even to the cutting off of hands and otherwise-mutilating the bodies of the victims. What are the yellow races to say to all this, especially in the face of complaints against the yellow peril? Can we be regarded as either unreasonable or unnecessarily offensive if we incline to the conviction that the peril is rather a white one?

Our American friends, who talk more about Freedom and Equality than most other nations, have nevertheless many hard things said of them by their own citizens in regard to their treatment of the Indians and Negroes. At any rate it would be difficult to parallel in any country in the East such savagery as the lynching and burning of negroes. According to the census of 1909 the negroes of 12 southern states made up 40% of the population; yet out of $32,000,000 spent in common school education in those states, only $4,000,000 went to the education of the coloured people, less than twelve and one half per cent of the total. Nor are conditions better in India, if we are to believe the accounts given by Englishmen themselves of the treatment of natives there. [. . .] Even the public conveniences are classified as for foreigners and natives; so that even the beggar and the outcast with white skin can be better accommodated than the most refined Indian gentleman. [. . .]

Now in the face of all this who can say that the yellow and otherwise coloured races are not in some peril from the white races? When I was on my way home from Europe there were some Englishmen on board the steamer, engineers on their way to posts in the Orient. Among these foreigners there seemed to prevail a very unpleasant degree of race-prejudice. Of their conduct toward the Chinese on board it is difficult to speak with due restraint. Once during the passage through the sultry heat of the tropics a Chinese gentleman of position came on deck to take a nap on a rattan chair. He had hardly got to sleep when he found himself wound round with coils of line and being dragged about the deck on his chair. This gentleman afterwards said to me: "Suppose the position were reversed, and it was a white man that was so treated, what would they say?" And then he went on to say that it was so everywhere, the white man always treating his yellow brother with contempt.

At the present time Australia is endeavoring to induce immigrants to settle in that country. Agents of the Commonwealth advertise endless acres of fertile land only awaiting people to occupy them. Even the passage money of prospective settlers is being advanced or paid by the government. The immigrants are promised every assistance in settling down, even to the loan of the necessary funds. Their children will be educated free in the national schools. Then the notice is conspicuously given that *only white people will be admitted.* [. . .] Practically the same attitude prevails in British South Africa, Canada, and the United States. Asiatics can enter only with the greatest inconvenience. [. . .]

Now from the point of view of the yellow races all this seems most arrogant and unfair. To seize the greater part of the earth and refuse to share with the races who are hardly pressed for territorial space at home, even when the privilege is highly paid for by hard labour, is so manifestly unjust that it cannot continue. [. . .] In Australia, South Africa, Canada and the United States there are vast tracts of unoccupied territory awaiting settlement, and although the citizens of the ruling powers refuse to take up the land, no yellow people are permitted to enter. [. . .] Thus the white races seem ready to commit to the savage beasts and birds what they refuse to entrust to their brothers of the yellow race. Even a yellow fisherman gleaning the sea along some solitary island coast is watched and apprehended for encroaching on the white preserves. Surely the arrogance and avarice of the nobility in appropriating to themselves the most and the best of the land in certain countries, is as nothing compared with the attitude of the white races toward those of a different hue. Suppose the conditions were reversed and the yellow races were thus territorially in the ascendancy! Suppose we enforced the same policy in, say, Korea or Manchuria! Well, I should not like to be responsible for the consequences. What an outcry there would be against "violation of equal opportunity" and the monopolization of natural resources. Well, the present attitude of the white races may be white, but it certainly is not Christian. Did not Christ say: "Do unto others as you would that they should do to you?" How can the white races have the face to demand equal opportunities in the East when they have denied them to the Far East in the West? It is a misfortune that we are not sufficiently Christianized to set about Christianizing the west in this particular! We do not pretend to be Christians, but we believe in doing unto others that we would have them do unto us!

Viewing the matter seriously, for it is a very serious matter indeed, it ought to be said that every defiance of justice must in the long run provoke revolt. Just as in the labour world, if the capitalist is unfair in his division of profits and the labourers are ground down, they will not forever submit, so the international world, unless justice obtains between race and race, there will be trouble. In the case under review, then, who will be responsible for the trouble? If one race assumes the right to appropriate all the wealth, why should not all the other races feel ill-used and protest? If the yellow races are oppressed by the white races, and have to revolt to avoid congestion and maintain existence, whose fault is it but that of the aggressors?

We freely admit that the yellow races cannot boast of any superlative innocence or achievement, though we furnished most of the religious inspiration and motive of the world. We have in some respects much to learn in the way of further advancement along modern lines. There are amongst us glaring deficiencies in culture and conspicuous inefficiencies of mechanical contrivance. But in morals we can compare favourably with those nations to whose aggression and greed we have with reluctance been obliged to allude. If our immigrants be honestly compared with those of other nations, we have nothing to fear. The average yellow immigrant entering the United States is found to possess a larger amount of capital than those from other countries. As nations the yellow people have never waged war of any kind on the white races, nor in any manner provoked them to jealousy or resentment. When we fight, it is always in self-defence. The white races preach to us, "peace, peace," and the futility and waste of armamental expansion; while all the time they are expending vast sums on armies and navies, and enforcing discrimination against us. Now, if the white races truly love peace, and wish to deserve the name of Christian nations, they will practice what they preach, and will soon restore to us the rights so long withheld. They will rise to the generosity of welcoming our citizens among them as heartily as we do theirs amongst us. To cry "peace, peace," without rendering us justice, is surely the hollowest of hypocrisy. Any suggestion that we must forever be content to remain inferior races, will not abide. Such an attitude is absolutely inconsistent with our honour as a nation and our sovereign rights as independent states. We therefore appeal to the white races to put aside their race-prejudice and meet us on equal terms in brotherly cooperation. This will convince us of their sincerity more quickly than a thousand proclamations of peace and good-will, while denying us sympathy and fair-play. Words and attitudes without charity are "as a sounding brass and a tinkling cymbal."

SAWAYANAGI MASATARŌ

From "Asianism," 1919

Sawayanagi Masatarō (1865–1927), a native of Nagano prefecture, graduated from Tokyo Imperial University in 1888. From 1888 to 1911 he worked in the Ministry of Education, where he helped unify and reform Japan's system of elementary education. Later he served as president of Tōhoku Imperial University in Sendai and Kyōto Imperial University. As chairman of the Imperial Conference for Education he attended a number of global conferences as Japan's representative.

In 1917, after retiring from his post at Kyōto Imperial University, Sawayanagi committed himself to promoting the cause of "cultural Asianism" and to call for the unity of what he called the "Asian race." Like many Japanese intellectuals, he was disappointed in the outcome of the Paris Peace Conference, where Western delegates—led by U.S. president Woodrow Wilson—blocked the inclusion of a clause in the peace treaty asserting the equality of all races. The result was a wave of anti-American sentiment in Japan; in one demonstration an activist went so far as to kill himself on the doorstep of the U.S. embassy in Tokyo. For Sawayanagi, Asianism was a viable alternative to the extremes of nationalism, on the one hand, and cosmopolitanism (as represented by the League of Nations) on the other.

SOURCE: *Sawayanagi Masatarō, "Asianism,"* The Japan Magazine, *1919, pp. 141–44.*

Asianism, as the word suggests, is not quite the same as cosmopolitanism: it is not so broad; neither is it so narrow as nationalism. The European Peace Conference [Paris Peace Conference, 1919] discusses such big problems as the elimination of race prejudice, and the League of Nations, but Asianism is not so ambitious as to include this. It involves principles that refer to the races of Asia only. It does not, however, conflict in any way with cosmopolitanism or any of the principles of humanity; it is only a process searching for certain high ideals.

Nationalism is concerned mainly with the things that pertain to certain countries, and cosmopolitanism deals with what pertains to all countries, but between these two comes racialism; and true nationalism can be understood only as we understand racialism. There are various opinions as to the meaning and significance of race. The Japanese race, for instance, includes the Yamato, the Korean, the Ainu and the Formosan races, yet not all of these belong to the Yamato race. [. . .] Thus race may be used sometimes in a broader or narrower sense. In the same way it is quite consistent to speak of all Asiatics as a race. In the same way we speak of the European race or the

African race. Though the Europeans are spoken of as a race there are many contradictions among them and they often make war on one another; yet they are sufficiently alike in blood, manners and customs and language to be called a race.

While the definition of race is thus left rather vague, that of nationality is rather clear; and many nations that can assert its independence and establish stable government is entitled to become a nation, however small. In the same way, the Japanese race is marked off by its possessions and territories and its frontiers are clearly defined. [. . .] As civilization advances cosmopolitanism takes greater hold upon the mind of man. The League of Nations is but one more example of this, and offers one of the biggest problems with which the human mind has had to deal. The same idea has been practised in a lesser way among various races and nationalities for a hundred years or more. We see it in international leagues, in the universal postal union, the Red Cross Society and the Churches to some extent. While races and nations are talking of the possibilities of the future, whether of peace or war, my mind runs toward racialism as the solution of the difficulty.

While thought may jump from one extreme to another, human activity can never afford to do so. Nations cannot change from extreme nationalism to extreme cosmopolitanism at a bound: they must pass first through a period of racialism. Asia has to go through its time of Asianism and Europe through its period of Europeanism, and perhaps America will finish with its Americanism too. All are trying to understand and to be understood. Misunderstanding is bad for trade and for the spirit too. That it does not cost us much thought is no sign of a condition to be proud of or satisfied with. There is even misunderstanding between the races of Asia, and this should give us profound concern and regret. Japan is of kindred race with China and India, and they are further united by religious and social bonds. Is it not very strange that we are trying to curry favour with western nations that have little in common with us? Not that we should be hostile to western nations but that we should be still more anxious to understand and know our neighbours of Asia. [. . .] While disapproving of the discrimination practised among western nations we must hasten to correct our own errors in this respect. No nation today is perfectly consistent in regard to equality of treatment among races. So long as there is undue distinction of classes there will be undue discrimination of races.

The spirit of democracy seems to be spreading over the entire world; but even in England and America, where the doctrine had birth and where it is most admired, is there any tendency to avoid extreme nationalism? This is clear from the proceedings of the [Paris] Peace Conference. The delegates of each nation are busy enforcing and maintaining their interests. It is obvious that great patriotism is not the monopoly of the Japanese. Among us democracy is also raising its voice and threatening to weaken our patriotism. But if my idea of racialism or Asianism were accepted and acted upon this untoward tendency would be corrected. [. . .] Our goal must be Asianism as the most important step on our way toward cosmopolitanism. Japan is the most advanced of all the countries of Asia, and she is conscious of her responsibility toward the rest of Asia. The peace of the Orient rests with Japan. She cannot be content to remain just as she is. Unless she is ready to pursue development still further in every branch of national activity she will not be able to realize her ideal of Asianism.

[. . .] Western nations are naturally afraid of orientals. The opposition of Premier Hughes of Australia shows this. When the Kaiser[1] invented the "yellow peril" bogey he unconsciously confessed western fear of Asia. This fear is a nightmare at the heart of western nations. If something is not done it may some day lead to a war between the East and the West; and the oriental people must be prepared for any such emergency. A federation of all the races of Asia will be the best way to do this: in other words, we must realize Asianism. [. . .]

Statement by the Amur Society (Kokuryūkai), 1930

Japan's first ultranationalist society, the Genyōsha, was formed by a group of former samurai in 1881. Horrified by the wholesale adoption of Western ideas by the Japanese government, and particularly by the decline of the country's traditional warrior class, the group became a dedicated enemy of liberalism. However, it promoted the cause of pan-Asianism by offering support to pro-Japanese revolutionary movements elsewhere in East Asia. In 1901 the group reformed itself as the Kokuryūkai (Amur Society, or, more literally, Black Dragon Society), named for the river that separates Russia from northeastern China, and dedicated itself primarily to promoting war with Russia. After World War I the group increasingly connected Pan-Asianism to domestic reform, bemoaning the plight of Japanese farmers and denouncing the zaibatsu as selfish and unpatriotic. The group published the following statement in recognition of its thirtieth anniversary.

SOURCE: *W. Theodore de Bary et al., eds.,* Sources of Japanese Tradition. *Volume Two: 1600–2000. Part Two: 1868–2000 (New York: Columbia University Press, 2006), pp. 263–65.*

Today our empire has entered a critical period in which great zeal is required on the part of the entire nation. From the first, we members of the Amur Society have worked in accordance with the imperial mission for overseas expansion to solve our overpopulation; at the same time, we have sought to give support and encouragement to the peoples of East Asia. Thus we

---

1. *Wilhelm II (1859–1941) was Kaiser [Emperor] of Germany from 1888 until his abdication in 1918, at the end of World War I. Although he did not coin the term "yellow peril," he promoted the idea heavily in an effort to encourage the European powers to collaborate in conquering and colonizing East Asia.*

have tried to spread humanity and righteousness throughout the world by having the imperial purpose extended to neighboring nations.

Earlier [as the Genyōsha], in order to achieve these principles, we organized the Heavenly Blessing Heroes[1] in Korea in 1894 and helped the Tong Hak rebellion[2] there in order to speed the settlement of the dispute between Japan and China. In 1899 we helped [Emilio] Aguinaldo[3] in his struggle for independence for the Philippines. In 1900 we worked with other comrades in helping Sun Yat-sen[4] start the fires of revolution in South China. In 1901 we organized this society and became exponents of the punishment of Russia, and thereafter we devoted ourselves to the annexation of Korea while continuing to support the revolutionary movement in China. At all times we have consistently centered our efforts on solving problems of foreign relations, and we have not spared ourselves in this cause.

During this period we have seen the fulfillment of our national power in the decisive victories in the two major wars against China and Russia, the annexation of Korea, the acquisition of Formosa and Sakhalin, and the expulsion of Germany from Shantung Peninsula. Japan's status among the empires of the world has risen until today it ranks as one of the three great powers, and from this eminence it can support other Asiatic nations. While these achievements were, of course, attributable to the august virtue of the great Meiji emperor, we cannot help but believe that our own efforts, however slight, also bore good fruit.

However, in viewing recent international affairs, it would seem that the foundation established by the great Meiji emperor is rapidly deteriorating. The disposition of the gains of the war with Germany was left to foreign powers, and the government, disregarding the needs of national defense, submitted to unfair demands to limit our naval power. Moreover, the failure of our China policy made

---

1. *The Heavenly Blessing Heroes* (Tenyūkyō) *were a group of Japanese volunteers who fought for Korea's independence from China.*

2. *Tong Hak is Korean for "eastern learning," a nationalistic, anti-Western religious movement that first emerged in Korea in 1860. The Tong Hak rebellion was an uprising in 1894 by Korean peasants inspired by this religion. When Chinese troops entered the country to suppress the rebellion, Japanese forces did likewise, and in the resulting Sino-Japanese War of 1894–95 Korea went from being a Chinese vassal state to a Japanese protectorate.*

3. *Emilio Aguinaldo (1869–1964) was a Filipino nationalist and revolutionary who led rebel forces against the Spanish in 1897–98. After the Spanish-American War, when the Philippines became a colony of the United States, Aguinaldo and his followers took up arms against U.S. troops. He was captured in 1901 and swore an oath of loyalty to the United States, at which point the insurrection came to an end.*

4. *Sun Yat-sen (1866–1925) was a Chinese physician and philosopher who led the revolution that overthrew the Qing dynasty in 1911. He was elected the first president of the Chinese Republic, but he soon stepped aside in favor of an army officer named Yuan Shikai. Yuan promptly tried to reestablish the empire—with himself as emperor—and drive Sun into exile in Japan. Yuan's regime quickly collapsed, and Sun returned to the country, but by then China had fallen into political chaos. He did not live to see the country's unification, which occurred under Jiang Jieshi.*

the Chinese more and more contemptuous of us, so much so that they have been brought to demand the surrender of our essential defense lines in Manchuria and Mongolia. Furthermore, in countries like the United States and Australia, our immigrants have been deprived of rights that were acquired only after long years of struggle, and we now face a high-handed anti-Japanese expulsion movement that knows no bounds. Men of purpose and of humanity who are at all concerned for their country cannot fail to be upset by the situation.

When we turn our attention to domestic affairs, we feel more than deep concern. There is a great slackening of discipline and order. Men's hearts are become corrupt. Look around you! Are not the various government measures and establishments a conglomeration of all sorts of evils and abuses? The laws are confusing, and evil grows apace. The people are overwhelmed by heavy taxes; the confusion in the business world has complicated the livelihood of the people; the growth of dangerous thought threatens social order; and our national polity, which has endured for three thousand years, is in danger. This is a critical time for our national destiny; was there ever a more crucial day? What else can we call this time if it is not to be termed decisive?

And yet, in spite of this, our government, instead of pursuing a farsighted policy, casts about for temporary measures. The opposition party simply struggles for political power without any notion of saving our country from this crisis. And even the press, which should devote itself to its duty of guiding and leading society, is the same. For the most part it swims with the current, bows to vulgar opinions, and is chiefly engrossed in moneymaking. Alas! Our empire moves ever closer to the rocks that lie before us! Truly, is this not the moment for us to become aroused?

Our determination to save the day is the inescapable consequences of this state of affairs. Previously our duty lay in the field of foreign affairs, but when we see internal affairs in disorder, how can we succeed abroad? Therefore we of the Amur Society have determined to widen the scope of our activity. Hereafter, besides our interest in foreign affairs, we will give unselfish criticism of internal politics and of social problems, and we will seek to guide public opinion into proper channels. Thereby we will, through positive action, continue in the tradition of our past. We will establish a firm basis for our organization's policy, and through cooperation with other groups devoted to similar political, social, and ideological ideals, we are resolved to reform the moral corruption of the people, restore social discipline, and ease the insecurity of the people's livelihood by relieving the crises in the financial world, restoring national confidence, and increasing the nation's strength, in order to carry out the imperial mission to awaken the countries of Asia. In order to clarify these principles, we here set forth our platform to all our fellow patriots:

PRINCIPLES

We stand for imperial rulership (*tennō shugi*). Basing ourselves on the fundamental teachings of the foundation of the empire, we seek the extension of the imperial influence to all peoples and places and the fulfillment of the glory of our national polity.

PLATFORM

1. Developing the great plan of the founders of the country, we will widen the great Way (*tao*) of Eastern culture, work out a harmony of Eastern and Western cultures, and take the lead among Asian peoples.

2. We will bring to an end many evils, such as formalistic legalism, which restricts the freedom of the people, hampers commonsense solutions, prevents efficiency in public and private affairs, and destroys the true meaning of constitutional government. Thereby we will show forth again the essence of the imperial principles.

3. We shall rebuild the present administrative system. We will develop overseas expansion through the activation of our diplomacy, further the prosperity of the people by reforms in internal government, and solve problems of labor and management by the establishment of new social policies. Thereby we will strengthen the foundations of the empire.

4. We shall carry out the spirit of the Imperial Rescript to Soldiers and Sailors and stimulate a martial spirit by working toward the goal of a nation in arms. Thereby we look toward the perfection of national defense.

5. We plan a fundamental reform of the present educational system, which is copied from those of Europe and the Americas; we shall set up a basic study of a national education originating in our national polity. Thereby we anticipate the further development and heightening of the wisdom and virtue of the Yamato race.

NAGAI RYŪTARŌ

From "Holy War for the Reconstruction of Asia," 1937

In 1920 Nagai Ryūtarō was elected to the Lower House of the Japanese Diet. As a loyal member of the Minseitō Party, he supported the liberal foreign policies of Shidehara Kijūrō, promoting trade with the West and friendship toward China. Nevertheless, he continued to criticize Americans and Europeans for their subjugation of non-whites around the world, and this likely helped him retain influence after the decline of civilian government in the early 1930s. In 1937, while serving as minister of communications in the first Konoe cabinet, Nagai gave the following speech defending Japan's campaign in China (which had begun that July), while insisting that it was directed against only the "Nanjing Government" (i.e., that of Jiang Jieshi) and not against the Chinese people.

SOURCE: *Sven Saaler and Christopher W. A. Szpilman, eds.,* Pan-Asianism: A Documentary History. Volume 2: *1920–Present (Lanham, MD: Rowman & Littlefield, 2011), pp. 156–59.*

Today [. . .] at the launching of the campaign for national spiritual mobilization, I join with all of you [. . .] participating in this profound national movement. As one who believes in the mission of the Japanese people, explaining our vital role in facilitating the opportunity for Asia's ascendance is a task after my own heart. [. . .] The purpose of this war is to crush the Nanking Government [of Jiang Jieshi] and all anti-Japanese resistance forces that support that regime and that, ignoring the joint mission of Japan and China for Oriental Peace (*Tūyō heiwa*), are attempting to expel Japan from China. In addition to realizing the spiritual and powerful union of the peoples of Japan and China who share this ideal of constructing a newly emergent Asia, it is clearly true that the purpose of the war rests in the establishment of eternal peace in the Orient. Although wars are common in the world, I believe just and fair motivation such as that which lies behind our current dispatch of troops to China is exceptional. On the occasion of opening the Seventy-second Diet Session, His Majesty proclaimed, "Our soldiers are sweeping aside all obstacles and through their fidelity and bravery will spur reflection on the part of Republican China and rapidly bring about none other than the establishment of peace in East Asia." Likewise, Prime Minister Konoe has on numerous occasions in the Diet declared that "what our country seeks in China is not territory but partnership." In short, what the Japanese people desire dearly is that the Chinese people return to their true Asian mind, through alliance with Japan establish Oriental Peace, and, via the establishment of Oriental Peace, contribute to world peace and the welfare of humanity. Among foreigners there are those who look at this war and viciously attack what they see as Japan's territorial ambitions in China—but if there are those who see in our contemporary dispatch of forces to China an action the same as England's earlier Opium War [1839–1842] [. . .] to forcefully import opium into China, or Russia's use of the Boxer Rising [1900] to plot the occupation of Manchuria [. . .] well, to put it in a nutshell, those people are exposing their own ignorance.

Reflecting back on the period after the Great War, one sees that the weak peoples of the world who were oppressed by the military and financial strength of the Great Powers responded to the great postwar collapse of that strength by raising flags of revolt, and that there arose suddenly a fierce current bearing their efforts to achieve self-liberation from imperialist control, brutal oppression, and exploitation and to thereby construct independent new states. The oppressed peoples of our Asian continent also moved to the fore by declaring independence and abandoning unequal treaties. As fellow Asians we Japanese cannot repress heartfelt feelings of respect at the addition of these glorious new pages to the history of Asia. However, at this very moment China [. . .] submits before the imperialist hegemony of foreign countries that differ from China and its cultural system. What is this ugly state of affairs whereby the Bolshevization and colonization of all of China is ignored? Upon consideration, one sees that this is the result of the Nanking Government and the Chinese ruling classes connected with it being blinded by their desire to maintain political power and, in order to do so, unhesitatingly colluding with any and all foreign powers. The existence of such a government is China's one great shame. The establishment of Oriental Peace is the consistent national policy of Japan, and if people truly desire to work for the establishment of Oriental Peace, they will strengthen the partnership of the peoples of Japan, Manchukuo and China, countries that are Asian and that share a common culture, and establish the grand principle of mutual aid in national defense and industry. There is no other path than to resist stoutly those foreign powers bearing ambitions to dominate Asia and to construct for Japan, Manchukuo and China a New World of co-prosperity that is absolutely devoid of exploitation. Therefore, our dispatch of troops to China is part of a war of Asian reconstruction aimed at eradicating the anti-Asian and anti-independence ideology of slavery of a Nanking Government that is working to reject and hinder the realization of this grand ideal.

Japan, reflecting its long-standing position of leadership in Asia, has exerted itself fully to aid China in building a new country independent and autonomous. In Peiping [present Beijing], at the opening of the Conference on Tariff Reform, Japan led the nations of the world in endeavoring to recognize Chinese tariff autonomy. Likewise, at the Commission on Repealing Extraterritoriality, Japan exerted tremendous effort to improve China's position and, already full of sympathy, looked forward eagerly to the day when China would be reborn as a unified state. Nevertheless, the Nanking Government not only fails to understand Japan's true intentions, they moreover use anti-Japanism as a means to unify China and preserve their own power. [. . .] This vehement cultivation of hatred for Japan among all Chinese is truly an outrage that will destroy the foundation for Oriental Peace. The existence of such a government is completely incompatible with the idea of world peace. As a consequence, in recent years the trend toward viewing Japan as the enemy has spread throughout China [and incidents of anti-Japanese violence have escalated]. [. . .] On average there is a victim every four days, with the climax being reached in this July's incident at the Marco Polo Bridge [the beginning Sino-Japanese War of 1937]. [. . .] Under these circumstances, resolutely and fearlessly striking a crushing blow against the Nanking Government and its military, thus depriving them completely of fighting spirit, and explaining thoroughly effective ways for preventing any repeat of such untoward incidents comprise Japan's mission for world peace and, at the same time, are an exercise of the Japanese people's inevitable right of self-defense.

However, the target Japan aims to strike is the Nanking Government and its military which continue implementing mistaken policies of anti-Japanese resistance—in no way is it the Chinese people. We of course bear no enmity toward the Chinese people; if anything, we cannot suppress our limitless sympathy for the Chinese people who, being oppressed by the Nanking Government and the foreign powers that pull its strings, even now are unable to achieve the true independence they so desire. [. . .] As Japanese, no matter what long-term resistance we confront, so long as the objectives of the Emperor's campaigning forces remain unattained, we must—with weapons in hand and with an uncompromising, indomitable and dauntless spirit—be resolved to continue the advance.

For this reason, as well as so as not to cause anxiety in the minds of those officers and men on the front lines, those on the home front must also exert themselves to the utmost in their respective posts. All the people must arise and each and every one must awaken to the grand historical mission of the Japanese Empire and work to fulfill their duties on the home front. At the time of the Great War, Germany was surrounded at its borders by some two million enemy troops yet continued fighting for five long years and never allowed one enemy soldier to set foot on German soil, something at which the world truly marveled. Under those circumstances, the strenuous efforts of Germans on the home front and their vigorous determination to sacrifice their lives for their country were in no way inferior to that of German soldiers on the battlefield. [. . .] Today the Japanese government, in order to comfort the families of deployed soldiers and raise public bonds, is seeking ardently the cooperation of Japanese on the home front in reducing unnecessary expenses, curtailing overseas payments by limiting consumption of foreign goods, and preserving domestic resources with military use by encouraging the use of substitute goods. Should the home front efforts of the Japanese people, who have been trained to lead through the grand spirit of patriotic devotion over the course of three thousand years, prove inferior to the German people in zeal, exertion and cooperation, the Japanese people would themselves bring shame upon Japanese culture. [. . .] Before the great purpose of national survival we must discard the narrow matters of the self and display our resolve to work for the greater good. Similarly, those Japanese on the home front through whose veins courses that grand spirit of patriotic devotion must teach the entire world that they are the equal of our officers and men fighting gallantly at the front. Ever since the occurrence of this incident, it is the brave and righteous actions of the officers and men of our army and navy on battlefields in north, central, and southern China that continue to surprise the world. Indeed, it is our national character tempered over three thousand years that, in the face of national crisis, emits a unique brilliance, and I believe it is on account of this unrivaled Japanese spirit that we display such profound *esprit* before the world. [. . .] In order to accomplish the task bequeathed by our ancestors we must exert ourselves strenuously so as to feel no shame before them, add yet more pages to the brilliant history of the glorious Japanese Empire, cultivate even more splendidly our proud national character, and feel keenly our heavy responsibility to pass this on to later generations. Should there be among Japanese charged with defending the home front those who do not awaken to this grave responsibility, who neglect their indispensable home-front duty to console the minds of officers and men giving their all at the front, and who begrudge cooperating with the current national campaign to realize Japan's historic mission in the world, one must say that such people relinquish their special rights as Japanese. When their time comes to die, I think they will be utterly unable to face our brave ancestors.

The point is that this war is not just the fight of the government, nor is it just the fight of the army and navy—truly it is the fight of all Japanese for the purpose of realizing the country's grand foundational ideal of *hakkō ichiu* ("the eight corners of the world under one roof") and a new world of human fraternity. Many will probably agree that the greatest source of instability in the world today is the widespread impoverishment accompanying the monopolization of resources in the international arena and the Bolshevik revolutionary schemes that, taking advantage of the resulting inequality and dissatisfaction, are being carried out around the globe. There is only one moral path that will liberate all of humanity from this global insecurity, reconstruct economic relations between nations on the basis of international justice, and lead to a world wherein all territory, capital, and labor are mobilized for the stable livelihood of all humanity. Namely, it is the moral mission of the Japanese people to carry forth the leadership principles for world reconstruction and, not just in the Orient but throughout the world, fight against exclusionism and communism. Therefore, this war—that is to say, Japan's eradication of exclusionist, communist forces in China—is truly the first step toward the moral and historical mission of realizing throughout the world *hakkō ichiu* and the great ideal of human fraternity.

MIYAZAKI MASAYOSHI

From "On the East Asian League," 1938

Born to a former samurai family from Kanazawa, Miyazaki Masayoshi (1897–1954) was studying Russian in St. Petersburg when the czarist regime was overthrown in March 1917. He left before the Bolshevik seizure of power that October, but his subsequent career would be shaped by these developments. Taking a job with the research section of the South Manchurian Railway, he became the company's resident expert on Soviet affairs. Although he had no fondness for Marxism, Miyazaki—like many of Japan's "reform bureaucrats"—admired the Soviet model of a centrally planned economy. After the Japanese occupation of Manchuria in 1931 he submitted a proposal calling for the development of heavy industry in the region largely on Soviet lines.

In 1937 Miyazaki, now in Tokyo on the staff of an army-based think tank called the Japan-Manchukuo Finance and Economics Research Association, proposed a plan for state-controlled development of Japan itself. The goal was to give Japan, within five years, the industrial power to face any of the more-developed powers of the West. His vision called for substantial government control of the economy and rigid controls on banks and other privately owned institutions. To his frustration, however, the immediate needs of the China Incident got in the way of his long-term projects. He also worried that to the Chinese and other peoples of East Asia the actions of the Japanese Army too closely resembled the methods of Western imperialism and might therefore undermine the appeal of Pan-Asianism. While the army naturally rejected this view, it became popular—along with Miyazaki's views on economic planning—among Japan's bureaucracy.

SOURCE: *Sven Saaler and Christopher W. A. Szpilman, eds.,* Pan-Asianism: A Documentary History. *Volume 2: 1920–Present (Lanham, MD: Rowman & Littlefield, 2011), pp. 182–83.*

The policy of an East Asian League means turning away from our emulation of European imperialist and colonial polices and eventually repudiating them. [. . .]

I cannot emphasize enough that, in abandoning our imperialist policies, our nation must not vacillate. Today, the ambition to justify all of Japan's deeds has a strong grip over the nation. A posture of ruthlessly defending every one of our policies in the past, however, does not demonstrate the magnanimity of a great nation. Although our continental policy brought peace and prosperity to Korea and achieved a perfect merger of the Japanese and Korean peoples, we should not lose sight of the fact that we have lost supporters for our policies in East Asia. Japan must revert to its own course. It must reestablish a position of leadership in East Asia. For this reason, it is essential that we drive out any vestiges of imperialist thought remaining in our public discourse. As long as these attitudes persist in Japan, it will be difficult for East Asians to grasp the East Asian League framework, but moreover its policies will lose their moral force. In this sense, Japan, as the advocate for the League, must investigate the psyche of oppressed peoples thoroughly at every stage of the League's formulation. We must be ever mindful that the structure of the League not replace the system of Western exploitation with a system of Japanese oppression and must further be resolved not to give the impression that it will.

With the League taking as its goal the liberation of East Asian peoples, the right of political independence of liberated peoples must be guaranteed unconditionally. As Japan and its allies cooperate with the liberation movements of other East Asian peoples, it must be left to voluntary decision whether they join the League or whether they remain completely independent nations. Further, we must recognize a right of withdrawal after joining. The East Asian League is a union of autonomous East Asian nations, which should be bound closely by the sinews of mutual political and economic interdependence between Japan and its allies. It is not a system of coercion. The ultimate will to independent statehood cannot be suppressed. I believe that, with Japan and its allies assuming this stance, centrifugal forces will be very weak and the chances of a people distancing themselves from the League would be extremely small. From the perspective of the development of national economies generally or from the perspective of the benefits for ordinary individuals, the fact is that advantage is gained by being part of a big nation or a big bloc. During this recent period of quasi-warfare among competing blocs, this holds especially true for a small, weak country in the corner of East Asia. The historical significance of an East Asian League to East Asians could be most easily understood were Japan to adopt such a stance. [. . .]

Miyazaki goes on ascribe the oppressive race relations under European empires to the liberal, free trade ideology of the West.

The White man's system of rule over East Asia was, at root, shot through with liberal thought. Those who think my words are extreme need look no further than the cases of natives of India, the Annamites of French Indochina, the blacks of South Africa or the present state of the blacks and native Indians of the United States. [. . .]

It is emotionally stunning to think back to the days before the Manchurian Incident—when a segment of the Japanese intelligentsia longed for free trade, held out hope for the potential of a global economy, and even advocated abandoning Manchuria—that the day had arrived when the thought and systems of Western liberalism held such potency that Japanese would abandon their own East Asianness (*Tōyōsei*). [. . .]

The establishment of an East Asian League is a comprehensive renovationist policy, combining the renovation of our policy on the continent with the establishment of a new domestic order. Its renovationist character becomes increasingly clear, as evidenced by our comprehensive global policy through the Anti-Comintern Pact [concluded with Germany in 1936], and presents powerful testimony that Japan is entering a new epoch.

ARITA HACHIRŌ

From "The International Situation and Japan's Position," 1940

Germany's stunning victories in Europe in spring 1940 presented new opportunities for Japan's leaders. With France and the Low Countries occupied by German troops, and Great Britain facing attacks by air and sea (and perhaps even an invasion), there seemed little chance that European powers could protect their colonies in East Asia from a determined Japanese effort to grab them. In this situation Foreign Minister Arita Hachirō proposed the creation of a "Greater East Asia Co-Prosperity Sphere" under Tokyo's leadership.

SOURCE: *Arita Hachirō, "The International Situation and Japan's Position," June 1940, in* Papers Relating to the Foreign Relations of the United States, Japan, 1931–1941, *vol. I (Washington, DC: U.S. Government Printing Office, 1943).*

Japan's ideal since foundation of the Empire has been that all nations should be enabled to find their proper places in [the] world. Our foreign policy has also been based upon this ideal, for which we have not hesitated at times even to fight by staking our national existence. What entire mankind longs for is firm establishment of world peace. But it goes without saying that peace can never endure unless it is a peace in which all nations enjoy their proper places. Unfortunately, however, establishment of world peace in this sense is difficult of speedy realization at [the] present stage of human progress. In order to realize such a great deal, therefore, it seems to be a most natural step that peoples who are closely related with each other geographically, racially, culturally, and economically should first form a sphere of their own for co-existence and co-prosperity and establish peace and order within that sphere, and at same time secure a relationship of common existence and prosperity with other spheres. The cause of strife which mankind has hitherto experienced lies generally in the failure to give due consideration to the necessity of some such natural and constructive world order and to remedy old irrationalities and injustices. The war in Europe brings home the truth of this with special emphasis. Therefore, in order to establish international peace on a permanent foundation every effort must be exerted for rectification of blunders that have been committed in this regard. It is in this spirit that Japan is now engaged in the task of establishing a new order in East Asia. [. . .] Countries of

East Asia and regions of the South Seas are geographically, historically, racially, and economically very closely related to each other. They are destined to help each other and minister to one another's needs for their common well-being and prosperity, and to promote peace and progress in their regions. Uniting of all these regions under a single sphere on the basis of common existence and insuring thereby the stability of that sphere is, I think, a natural conclusion. The idea to establish first a righteous peace in each of the various regions and then establish collectively a just peace for the whole world has long existed also in Europe and America. This system presupposes the existence of a stabilizing force in each region, with which as a center the peoples within that region are to secure their co-existence and co-prosperity and as well the stability of their sphere. It also presupposes that these groups will respect another's individual characteristics, political, cultural, and economic, and they will cooperate and fulfill one another's needs for their common good. When the present European war broke out, the Japanese Government at once declared their policy [of] non-involvement and made it clear that this country did not intend to intervene in Europe and at the same time did not want to see the war spread into East Asia. Quite naturally Japan expects that Eastern [*Western*] powers will do nothing that will exert any undesirable influence upon the stability of East Asia. Japan, while carrying on vigorously her task of constructing a new order in East Asia, is paying serious attention to developments in the European war and to its repercussions in the various quarters of East Asia, including the South Seas region. I desire to declare that the destiny of these regions in any development therein, and any disposal thereof, is a matter for grave concern to Japan in view of her mission and responsibility as the stabilizing force in East Asia.

SUPPLEMENTAL DOCUMENTS

The Constitution of the Empire of Japan, 1889

Commonly referred to as the "Meiji Constitution," Japan's first written constitution was drafted largely by the country's first prime minister, Itō Hirobumi, who chaired a commission of legal experts that studied similar charters from around the world. The U.S. Constitution was rejected as too liberal, but that of Spain was regarded as too despotic. In the end the commission chose the model of Prussia's constitution (which also formed the basis for the constitution of the German Empire), but affirmed the divine nature of the emperor. The Meiji emperor promulgated the constitution in February 1889, but it did not take effect until the following year.

SOURCE: *The Constitution of Japan: With the Laws Pertaining Thereto, and the Imperial Oath and Speech. Promulgated at the Imperial Palace, February 11th, 1889, Japan Gazette, 1889, pp. 1–5.*

IMPERIAL OATH SWORN IN THE SANCTUARY IN THE IMPERIAL PALACE

We, the Successor to the prosperous Throne of Our Predecessors, do humbly and solemnly swear to the Imperial Founder of Our House and to Our other Imperial Ancestors that, in pursuance of a great policy co-extensive with the Heavens and with the Earth, We shall maintain and secure from decline the ancient form of government.

In consideration of the progressive tendency of the course of human affairs and in parallel with the advance of civilization, We deem it expedient, in order to give clearness and distinctness to the instructions bequeathed by the Imperial Founder of Our House and by Our other Imperial Ancestors, to establish fundamental laws formulated into express provisions of law, so that, on the one hand, Our Imperial posterity may possess an express guide for the course they are to follow, and that, on the other, Our subjects shall thereby be enabled to enjoy a wider range of action in giving Us their support, and that the observance of Our laws shall continue to the remotest ages of time. We will thereby to give greater firmness to the stability of Our country and to promote the welfare of all the people within the boundaries of Our dominions; and We now establish the Imperial House Law and the Constitution. These Laws come to only an exposition of grand precepts for the conduct of the government, bequeathed by the Imperial Founder of Our House and by Our other Imperial Ancestors. That we have been so fortunate in Our reign, in keeping with the tendency of the times, as to accomplish this work, We owe to the glorious Spirits of the Imperial Founder of Our House and of Our other Imperial Ancestors.

We now reverently make Our prayer to Them and to Our Illustrious Father, and implore the help of Their Sacred Spirits, and make to Them solemn oath never at this time nor in the future to fail to be an example to our subjects in the observance of the Laws hereby established.

May the heavenly Spirits witness this Our solemn Oath.

IMPERIAL RESCRIPT ON THE PROMULGATION OF THE CONSTITUTION

Whereas We make it the joy and glory of Our heart to behold the prosperity of Our country, and the welfare of Our subjects, We do hereby, in virtue of the Supreme power We inherit from Our Imperial Ancestors, promulgate the present immutable fundamental law, for the sake of Our present subjects and their descendants.

The Imperial Founder of Our House and Our other Imperial ancestors, by the help and support of the forefathers of Our subjects, laid the foundation of Our Empire upon a basis, which is to last forever. That this brilliant achievement embellishes the annals of Our country, is due to the glorious virtues of Our Sacred Imperial ancestors, and to the loyalty and bravery of Our subjects, their love of their country and their public spirit. Considering that Our subjects are the descendants of the loyal and good subjects of Our Imperial Ancestors, We doubt not but that Our subjects will be guided by Our views, and will sympathize with all Our endeavors, and that, harmoniously cooperating together, they will share with Us Our hope of making manifest the glory of Our country, both at home and abroad, and of securing forever the stability of the work bequeathed to Us by Our Imperial Ancestors.

PREAMBLE [OR EDICT] (JOYU)

Having, by virtue of the glories of Our Ancestors, ascended the throne of a lineal succession unbroken for ages eternal; desiring to promote the welfare of, and to give development to the moral and intellectual faculties of Our beloved subjects, the very same that have been favored with the benevolent care and affectionate vigilance of Our Ancestors; and hoping to maintain the prosperity of the State, in concert with Our people and with their support, We hereby promulgate, in pursuance of Our Imperial Rescript of the 12th day of the 10th month of the 14th year of Meiji, a fundamental law of the State, to exhibit the principles, by which We are guided in Our conduct, and to point out to what Our descendants and Our subjects and their descendants are forever to conform.

The right of sovereignty of the State, We have inherited from Our Ancestors, and We shall bequeath them to Our descendants. Neither We nor they shall in the future fail to wield them, in accordance with the provisions of the Constitution hereby granted.

We now declare to respect and protect the security of the rights and of the property of Our people, and to secure to them the complete enjoyment of the same, within the extent of the provisions of the present Constitution and of the law.

The Imperial Diet shall first be convoked for the 23rd year of Meiji and the time of its opening shall be the date when the present Constitution comes into force.

When in the future it may become necessary to amend any of the provisions of the present Constitution, We or Our successors shall assume the initiative right, and submit a project for the same to the Imperial Diet. The Imperial Diet shall pass its vote upon it, according to the conditions imposed by the present Constitution, and in no otherwise shall Our descendants or Our subjects be permitted to attempt any alteration thereof.

Our Ministers of State, on Our behalf, shall be held responsible for the carrying out of the present Constitution, and Our present and future subjects shall forever assume the duty of allegiance to the present Constitution.

CHAPTER I: THE EMPEROR

Article 1. The Empire of Japan shall be reigned over and governed by a line of Emperors unbroken for ages eternal.

Article 2. The Imperial Throne shall be succeeded to by Imperial male descendants, according to the provisions of the Imperial House Law.

Article 3. The Emperor is sacred and inviolable.

Article 4. The Emperor is the head of the Empire, combining in Himself the rights of sovereignty, and exercises them, according to the provisions of the present Constitution.

Article 5. The Emperor exercises the legislative power with the consent of the Imperial Diet.

Article 6. The Emperor gives sanction to laws, and orders them to be promulgated and executed.

Article 7. The Emperor convokes the Imperial Diet, opens, closes, and prorogues it, and dissolves the House of Representatives.

Article 8. The Emperor, in consequence of an urgent necessity to maintain public safety or to avert public calamities, issues, when the Imperial Diet is not sitting, Imperial ordinances in the place of law.

Such Imperial Ordinances are to be laid before the Imperial Diet at its next session, and when the Diet does not approve the said Ordinances, the Government shall declare them to be invalid for the future.

Article 9. The Emperor issues or causes to be issued, the Ordinances necessary for the carrying out of the laws, or for the maintenance of the public peace and order, and for the promotion of the welfare of the subjects. But no Ordinance shall in any way alter any of the existing laws.

Article 10. The Emperor determines the organization of the different branches of the administration, and salaries of all civil and military officers, and appoints and dismisses the same. Exceptions especially provided for in the present Constitution or in other laws, shall be in accordance with the respective provisions (bearing thereon).

Article 11. The Emperor has the supreme command of the Army and Navy.

Article 12. The Emperor determines the organization and peace standing of the Army and Navy.

Article 13. The Emperor declares war, makes peace, and concludes treaties.

Article 14. The Emperor declares a state of siege. The conditions and effects of a state of siege shall be determined by law.

Article 15. The Emperor confers titles of nobility, rank, orders and other marks of honor.

Article 16. The Emperor orders amnesty, pardon, commutation of punishments and rehabilitation.

Article 17. A Regency shall be instituted in conformity with the provisions of the Imperial House Law. The Regent shall exercise the powers appertaining to the Emperor in His name.

CHAPTER II: RIGHTS AND DUTIES OF SUBJECTS

Article 18. The conditions necessary for being a Japanese subject shall be determined by law.

Article 19. Japanese subjects may, according to qualifications determined in laws or ordinances, be appointed to civil or military or any other public offices equally.

Article 20. Japanese subjects are amenable to service in the Army or Navy, according to the provisions of law.

Article 21. Japanese subjects are amenable to the duty of paying taxes, according to the provisions of law.

Article 22. Japanese subjects shall have the liberty of abode and of changing the same within the limits of the law.

Article 23. No Japanese subject shall be arrested, detained, tried or punished, unless according to law.

Article 24. No Japanese subject shall be deprived of his right of being tried by the judges determined by law.

Article 25. Except in the cases provided for in the law, the house of no Japanese subject shall be entered or searched without his consent.

Article 26. Except in the cases mentioned in the law, the secrecy of the letters of every Japanese subject shall remain inviolate.

Article 27. The right of property of every Japanese subject shall remain inviolate. Measures necessary to be taken for the public benefit shall be any provided for by law.

Article 28. Japanese subjects shall, within limits not prejudicial to peace and order, and not antagonistic to their duties as subjects, enjoy freedom of religious belief.

Article 29. Japanese subjects shall, within the limits of law, enjoy the liberty of speech, writing, publication, public meetings and associations.

Article 30. Japanese subjects may present petitions, by observing the proper forms of respect, and by complying with the rules specially provided for the same.

Article 31. The provisions contained in the present Chapter shall not affect the exercises of the powers appertaining to the Emperor, in times of war or in cases of a national emergency.

Article 32. Each and every one of the provisions contained in the preceding Articles of the present Chapter, that are not in conflict with the laws or the rules and discipline of the Army and Navy, shall apply to the officers and men of the Army and of the Navy.

CHAPTER III: THE IMPERIAL DIET

Article 33. The Imperial Diet shall consist of two Houses, a House of Peers and a House of Representatives.

Article 34. The House of Peers shall, in accordance with the ordinance concerning the House of Peers, be composed of the members of the Imperial Family, of the orders of nobility, and of those who have been nominated thereto by the Emperor.

Article 35. The House of Representatives shall be composed of members elected by the people, according to the provisions of the law of Election.

Article 36. No one can at one and the same time be a Member of both Houses.

Article 37. Every law requires the consent of the Imperial Diet.

Article 38. Both Houses shall vote upon projects of law submitted to it by the Government, and may respectively initiate projects of law.

Article 39. A Bill, which has been rejected by either the one or the other of the two Houses, shall not be brought in again during the same session.

Article 40. Both Houses can make representations to the Government, as to laws or upon any other subject. When, however, such representations are not accepted, they cannot be made a second time during the same session.

Article 41. The Imperial Diet shall be convoked every year.

Article 42. A session of the Imperial Diet shall last during three months. In case of necessity, the duration of a session may be prolonged by the Imperial Order.

Article 43. When urgent necessity arises, an extraordinary session may be convoked in addition to the ordinary one. The duration of an extraordinary session shall be determined by Imperial Order.

Article 44. The opening, closing, prolongation of session and prorogation of the Imperial Diet, shall be effected simultaneously for both Houses. In case the House of Representatives has been ordered to dissolve, the House of Peers shall at the same time be prorogued.

Article 45. When the House of Representatives has been ordered to dissolve, Members shall be caused by Imperial Order to be newly elected, and the new House shall be convoked within five months from the day of dissolution.

Article 46. No debate can be opened and no vote can be taken in either House of the Imperial Diet, unless not less than one-third of the whole number of Members thereof is present.

Article 47. Votes shall be taken in both Houses by absolute majority. In the case of a tie vote, the President shall have the casting vote.

Article 48. The deliberations of both Houses shall be held in public. The deliberations may, however, upon demand of the Government or by resolution of the House, be held in secret sitting.

Article 49. Both Houses of the Imperial Diet may respectively present addresses to the Emperor.

Article 50. Both Houses may receive petitions presented by subjects.

Article 51. Both Houses may enact, besides what is provided for in the present Constitution and in the Law of the Houses, rules necessary for the management of their internal affairs.

Article 52. No Member of either House shall be held responsible outside the respective Houses, for any opinion uttered or for any vote given in the House. When, however, a Member himself has given publicity to his opinions by public speech, by documents in print or in writing, or by any other similar means, he shall, in the matter, be amenable to the general law.

Article 53. The Members of both Houses shall, during the session, be free from arrest, unless with the consent of the House, except in cases of flagrant delicts, or of offenses connected with a state of internal commotion or with a foreign trouble.

Article 54. The Ministers of State and the Delegates of the Government may, at any time, take seats and speak in either House.

CHAPTER IV: THE MINISTERS OF STATE AND THE PRIVY COUNCIL

Article 55. The respective Ministers of State shall give their advice to the Emperor, and be responsible for it. All Laws, Imperial Ordinances, and Imperial Rescripts of whatever kind, that relate to the affairs of the state, require the countersignature of a Minister of State.

Article 56. The Privy Councillors shall, in accordance with the provisions for the organization of the Privy Council, deliberate upon important matters of State when they have been consulted by the Emperor.

CHAPTER V: THE JUDICATURE

Article 57. The Judicature shall be exercised by the Courts of Law according to law, in the name of the Emperor. The organization of the Courts of Law shall be determined by law.

Article 58. The judges shall be appointed from among those, who possess proper qualifications according to law. No judge shall be deprived of his position, unless by way of criminal sentence or disciplinary punishment. Rules for disciplinary punishment shall be determined by law.

Article 59. Trials and judgments of a Court shall be conducted publicly. When, however, there exists any fear, that such publicity may be prejudicial to peace and order, or to the maintenance of public morality, the public trial may be suspended by provisions of law or by the decision of the Court of Law.

Article 60. All matters that fall within the competency of a special Court, shall be specially provided for by law.

Article 61. No suit at law, which relates to rights alleged to have been infringed by the illegal measures of the administrative authorities, and which shall come within the competency of the Court of Administrative Litigation specially established by law, shall be taken cognizance of by Court of Law.

CHAPTER VI: FINANCE

Article 62. The imposition of a new tax or the modification of the rates (of an existing one) shall be determined by law. However, all such administrative fees or other revenue having the nature of compensation shall not fall within the category of the above clause. The raising of national loans and the contracting of other liabilities to the charge of the National Treasury, except those that are provided in the Budget, shall require the consent of the Imperial Diet.

Article 63. The taxes levied at present shall, in so far as they are not remodelled by a new law, be collected according to the old system.

Article 64. The expenditure and revenue of the State require the consent of the Imperial Diet by means of an annual Budget. Any and all expenditures overpassing the appropriations set forth in the Titles and Paragraphs of the Budget, or that are not provided for in the Budget, shall subsequently require the approbation of the Imperial Diet.

Article 65. The Budget shall be first laid before the House of Representatives.

Article 66. The expenditures of the Imperial House shall be defrayed every year out of the National Treasury, according to the present fixed amount for the same, and shall not require the consent thereto of the Imperial Diet, except in case an increase thereof is found necessary.

Article 67. Those already fixed expenditures based by the Constitution upon the powers appertaining to the Emperor, and such expenditures as may have arisen by the effect of law, or that appertain to the legal obligations of the Government, shall be neither rejected nor reduced by the Imperial Diet, without the concurrence of the Government.

Article 68. In order to meet special requirements, the Government may ask the consent of the Imperial Diet to a certain amount as a Continuing Expenditure Fund, for a previously fixed number of years.

Article 69. In order to supply deficiencies, which are unavoidable, in the Budget, and to meet requirements unprovided for in the same, a Reserve Fund shall be provided in the Budget.

Article 70. When the Imperial Diet cannot be convoked, owing to the external or internal condition of the country, in case of urgent need for the maintenance of public safety, the Government may take all necessary financial measures, by means of an Imperial Ordinance. In the case mentioned in the preceding clause, the matter shall be submitted to the Imperial Diet at its next session, and its approbation shall be obtained thereto.

Article 71. When the Imperial Diet has not voted on the Budget, or when the Budget has not been brought into actual existence, the Government shall carry out the Budget of the preceding year.

Article 72. The final account of the expenditures and revenues of the State shall be verified and confirmed by the Board of Audit, and it shall be submitted by the Government to the Imperial Diet, together with the report of verification of the said board. The organization and competency of the Board of Audit shall of determined by law separately.

CHAPTER VII: SUPPLEMENTARY RULES

Article 73. When it has become necessary in future to amend the provisions of the present Constitution, a project to the effect shall be submitted to the Imperial Diet by Imperial Order. In the above case, neither House can open the debate, unless not less than two-thirds of the whole number of Members are present, and no amendment can be passed, unless a majority of not less than two-thirds of the Members present is obtained.

Article 74. No modification of the Imperial House Law shall be required to be submitted to the deliberation of the Imperial Diet. No provision of the present Constitution can be modified by the Imperial House Law.

Article 75. No modification can be introduced into the Constitution, or into the Imperial House Law, during the time of a Regency.

Article 76. Existing legal enactments, such as laws, regulations, Ordinances, or by whatever names they may be called, shall, so far as they do not conflict with the present Constitution, continue in force. All existing contracts or orders, that entail obligations upon the Government, and that are connected with expenditure, shall come within the scope of Article 67.

U.S. SECRETARY OF STATE JOHN HAY

The "Open Door Note," 1899

When at the end of the nineteenth century Japan and the European powers seemed poised to divide China into spheres of influence, U.S. Secretary of State John Hay sent the following note to France, Germany, Britain, Italy, Japan, and Russia. In it he requested a promise not to interfere with China's sovereignty or territorial integrity and to allow all countries to export goods to all parts of China on equal terms.

Hay's note was not taken particularly seriously at the time, and each recipient responded evasively. However, the principle of the "open door" in China would form the basis for U.S. policy in East Asia throughout the twentieth century.

SOURCE: *J. N. Larned, ed.,* History for Ready Reference from the Best Historians, Biographers, and Specialists, *vol. VI (Springfield, MA: The C. A. Nichols Co., 1901), p. 102.*

At the time when the Government of the United States was informed by that of Germany that it had leased from His Majesty the Emperor of China the port of Kiao-chao [Jiaozhou] and the adjacent territory in the province of Shantung, assurances were given to the ambassador of the United States at Berlin by the Imperial German minister for foreign affairs that the rights and privileges insured by treaties with China to citizens of the United States would not thereby suffer or be in anywise impaired within the area over which Germany had thus obtained control.

More recently, however, the British Government recognized by a formal agreement with Germany the exclusive right of the latter country to enjoy in said leased area and the contiguous "sphere of influence or interest" certain privileges, more especially those relating to railroads and mining enterprises; but as the exact nature and extent of the rights thus recognized have not been clearly defined, it is possible that serious conflicts of interest may at any time arise not only between British and German subjects within said area, but that the interests of our citizens may also be jeopardized thereby.

Earnestly desirous to remove any cause of irritation and to insure at the same time to the commerce of all nations in China the undoubted benefits which should accrue from a formal recognition by the various powers claiming "spheres of interest" that they shall enjoy perfect equality of treatment for their commerce and navigation within such "spheres," the Government of the United States would be pleased to see His German Majesty's Government give formal assurances, and lend its cooperation in securing like assurances from the other interested powers, that each, within its respective sphere of whatever influence—

First. Will in no way interfere with any treaty port or any vested interest within any so-called "sphere of interest" or leased territory it may have in China.

Second. That the Chinese treaty tariff of the time being shall apply to all merchandise landed or shipped to all such ports as are within said "sphere of interest" (unless they be "free ports"), no matter to what nationality it may belong, and that duties so leviable shall be collected by the Chinese Government.

Third. That it will levy no higher harbor dues on vessels of another nationality frequenting any port in such "sphere" than shall be levied on vessels of its own nationality, and no higher railroad charges over lines built, controlled, or operated within its "sphere" on merchandise belonging to citizens or subjects of other nationalities transported through such "sphere" than shall be levied on similar merchandise belonging to its own nationals transported over equal distances.

The liberal policy pursued by His Imperial German Majesty in declaring Kiaochao a free port and in aiding the Chinese Government in the establishment there of a custom-house are so clearly in line with the proposition which this Government is anxious to see recognized that it entertains the strongest hope that Germany will give its acceptance and hearty support.

The recent ukase of His Majesty the Emperor of Russia declaring the port of Ta-lien-wan [Dalian] open during the whole of the lease under which it is held from China to the merchant ships of all nations, coupled with the categorical assurances made to this Government by His Imperial Majesty's representative at this capital at the time and since repeated to me by the present Russian ambassador, seem to insure the support of the Emperor to the proposed measure. Our ambassador at the Court of St. Petersburg has in consequence been instructed to submit it to the Russian Government and to request their early consideration of it. [. . .]

The commercial interests of Great Britain and Japan will be so clearly served by the desired declaration of intentions, and the views of the Governments of these countries as to the desirability of the adoption of measures insuring the benefits of equality of treatment of all foreign trade throughout China are so similar to those entertained by the United States, that their acceptance of the propositions herein outlined and their cooperation in advocating their adoption by the other powers can be confidently expected. [. . .]

KONOE FUMIMARO

"Against a Pacifism Centered on England and America," 1918

Konoe Fumimaro (1891–1945), the scion of an ancient aristocratic family, served as prime minister during the outbreak of war with China in 1937 and later during the negotiations with the United States in 1941. He inherited a seat in the House of Peers from his father, Konoe Atsumaro, an ardent nationalist who had argued for a strong stance toward Russia on the eve of the Russo-Japanese War. In 1918 Konoe Fumimaro was appointed as a member of the Japanese delegation to the Paris Peace Conference. The following is an English-language paraphrase of an essay written on the eve of his departure. It expresses a view of the world shared by many Japanese political and military leaders of his generation, who had grown up in a Japan that had emerged as a major world power but whose people still faced racial discrimination abroad.

SOURCE: J. B. Powell, "Editorial Paragraphs," *Millard's Review of the Far East* VII:6 (January 11, 1919), p. 194.

The European war was a conflict between Powers in being and Powers to come, that is to say, between countries that considered it advantageous to maintain the status quo and those that thought it convenient to destroy the existing state of things. The former advocated peace and the latter war. It cannot be said that the advocates of peace always act in conformity with justice and humanity, while those favoring war are necessarily their violators. [. . .] [S]upposing the condition in Europe before the war was perfect the disturber of it would be justly called the enemy to the cause of humanity and justice. But if the contrary was the fact the disturber of peace cannot necessarily be the enemy of humanity, and the nations that endeavored to maintain the status quo have no qualifications to be proud of their attitude. No doubt the condition before the war was satisfactory from the viewpoint of Great Britain and America, but it cannot be said so, when considered from the viewpoint of justice and humanity. As may be seen in their history of colonization England and France occupied most of less civilized countries long ago and made them their colonies. In consequence Germany and other latecomers could hardly find-any land to secure for their expansion. This state of things was contrary to the fundamental principle of equal opportunity and a menace to the right of equal existence of different countries. [. . .] [I consider] it just and right for Germany to have tried to destroy this state of things. [. . .] [I do] not endorse the measures taken by her, but [express] sympathy for her in the position which compelled her to act as she did. In short, the British and American principle for peace was the same as that advocated by those desirous of maintaining the status quo and had no connection whatever with the principles of humanity and justice. Nevertheless, Japanese, enchanted by the beautiful and high-sounding words uttered by British and American statesmen in their declarations, have been misled to thinking that peace is equal to justice, and in spite of Japan being in a position like Germany to wish for the destruction of the status quo, are drunk with an Anglo-American peace welcoming the idea of a League of Nations like a heaven sent gospel. This attitude of the Japanese people is ignoble and greatly to be detested.

KITA IKKI

From "An Outline Plan for the Reorganization of Japan," 1919

Author Kita Ikki (1883–1937) was undoubtedly the most influential thinker among Japan's ultranationalists. His work, a blend of Western radicalism and traditional Asian thought, advocated an internal policy of radical reform and a foreign policy in which Japan assumed leadership of East Asia in a grand struggle against Western imperialism. Although he played no direct role in the uprising of February 1936, the rebels were clearly influenced by his work, so much so that Kita was arrested, tried, and executed for treason.

SOURCE: *W. Theodore de Bary et al., eds., trans. Marius Jansen,* Sources of Japanese Tradition. *Volume Two: 1600–2000. Part Two: 1868–2000 (New York: Columbia University Press, 2006), pp. 273–75.*

At Present the Japanese empire is faced with a national crisis unparalleled in its history; it faces dilemmas at home and abroad. The vast majority of the people feel insecure in their livelihood and are on the point of taking a lesson from the collapse of European societies, while those who monopolize political, military, and economic power simply hide themselves and, quaking with fear, try to maintain their unjust position. Abroad, not England, America, Germany, or Russia has kept its word, and even our neighbour China, which long benefited from the protection we provided through the Russo-Japanese War, not only has failed to repay us but instead despises us. Truly, we are a small island, completely isolated in the Eastern Sea. One false step and our nation will again fall into the desperate state of crisis—dilemmas at home and abroad—that marked the period before and after the Meiji Restoration.

The only thing that brightens the picture is the 60 million fellow countrymen with whom we are blessed. The Japanese people must develop a profound awareness of the great causes of national existence and of the people's equal rights, and they need an unerring, discriminating grasp of the complexities of domestic and foreign thought. The Great War in Europe was, like Noah's Flood, Heaven's punishment on them for arrogant and rebellious ways. [. . .]

Truly, our 700 million brothers in China and India have no path to independence other than that offered by our guidance and protection. [. . .] At a time when the authorities in European and American revolutionary creeds have found it completely impossible to arrive at an understanding of the "gospel of the sword" because of their superficial philosophy, the noble Greece of Asian culture must complete its national reorganization on the basis of its own national polity. At the same time, let it lift the virtuous banner of an Asian league and take the leadership in the world federation that must come. In so doing let it proclaim to the world the Way of Heaven in which all are children of Buddha, and let it set an example that the world must follow.

SECTION 1: THE PEOPLE'S EMPEROR

Suspension of the Constitution. In order for the emperor and the entire Japanese people to establish a secure base for the national reorganization, the emperor will, by a show of his imperial prerogative, suspend the constitution for a period of three years, dissolve both houses of the Diet, and place the entire nation under martial law.

(Note: In extraordinary times the authorities should, of course, ignore harmful opinions and votes. To regard any sort of constitution or parliament as an absolute authority is to act in direct imitation of the English and American semisacred "democracy." [. . .] It cannot be held that in the discussion of plans for naval expansion Admiral Tōgō [Heihachirō]'s vote was not worth more than the three cast by miserable members of the Diet.) [. . .]

(Note: A coup d'état should be regarded as a direct manifestation of the authority of the nation, that is, of the will of society. All the progressive leaders have arisen from popular groups. They arise because of political leaders like Napoleon and Lenin. In the reorganization of Japan there must be a manifestation of the power inherent in a coalition of the people and sovereign.) [. . .]

The True Significance of the Emperor. The fundamental doctrine of the emperor as representative of the people and as the pillar of the nation must be made clear.

In order to clarify this, sweeping reform of the imperial court in the spirit of the Emperor Jinmu in founding the state and in the spirit of the great Meiji emperor will be carried out. The present privy councillors and other officials will be dismissed from their posts and, in their place, will come talent, sought throughout the realm, capable of assisting the emperor. [. . .]

(Note: Japan's national polity has evolved through three stages, and the meaning of "emperor" has also evolved through three stages. The first stage, from the Fujiwara to the Taira, was one of absolute monarchy. During this stage the emperor possessed all land and people as his private property in theory, and he had the power of life and death over the people. The second stage, from the Minamoto to the Tokugawa, was one of aristocracy. During this period military leaders and nobility in each area brought land and people of their locality under their personal control. [. . .] The third stage, one of a democratic state, began with the Meiji Revolution, which emancipated the samurai and commoners, newly awakened, from their status as the private property of their shogun and feudal lords. Since then, the emperor has a new significance as the true center of government and politics. Ever since, as the commanding figure in the national movement and as the overall representative of the nation. In other words, since the Meiji Revolution, Japan has become a modern democratic state with the emperor as its political nucleus. Is there any need whatsoever for us to import a direct translation of the "democracy" of others as though we lacked something?) [. . .]

(Note: There is no scientific basis whatsoever for the belief of the democracies that a state governed by representatives voted in by the electorate is superior to a state with a system of government by a particular person. Every nation has its own national spirit and history. [. . .] The "democracy" of Americans derives from the very unsophisticated theory of the time, which held that society can come into being through a voluntary contract based on the free will of individuals; these people, emigrating from each European country as individuals, established communities and built a country. But their theory of the divine right of voters is a half-witted philosophy that arose in opposition to the theory of the divine right of kings at that time. Now Japan certainly was not founded in this way, and there has never been a period in which Japan was dominated by a half-witted philosophy. Suffice it to say that the system whereby the head of state has to struggle for election by a long-winded self-advertisement and by exposing himself to ridicule like a low-class actor seems a very strange custom to the Japanese people, who have been brought up in the belief that silence is golden and modesty is a virtue.) [. . .]

The Abolition of the Peerage System. The peerage system will be abolished, and the spirit of the Meiji Restoration will be clarified by removing the barrier that has come between the emperor and the people.

SŌBUN YAMAMURO

Excerpts from a Speech, 1929

Sōbun Yamamuro was an executive for Mitsubishi, one of the most powerful of Japan's zaibatsu. His views reflect the widespread support for "Shidehara diplomacy" among the business community in the 1920s.

SOURCE: *W. Theodore de Bary et al., eds.,* Sources of Japanese Tradition. *Volume Two: 1600–2000. Part Two: 1868–2000 (New York: Columbia University Press, 2006), pp. 210–11.*

When we consider [the state] of Japan's national economy, when we think of our scarcity of natural resources, when we reflect upon today's international situation, [the solution to our problems might seem to lie in] either the seizure of dependencies under a policy of aggression or the establishment of a Monroe Doctrine. Nevertheless, there is absolutely no place in Japan's future for [these policies]. Japan can keep itself a going concern only by means of international cooperation. Under this policy of international cooperation we can get along by producing goods of the highest possible quality at the lowest possible price, thereby expanding our foreign markets to the greatest [extent] possible. A country as deficient in natural resources as Japan buys raw materials from foreign countries at low prices and processes [these materials] at a low cost. Of course, circumstances peculiar to Japan have [modified] our development. For example, silk has been an important item. However, in addition to encouraging the expansion of this industry we must endeavor through a policy of international cooperation to establish our country as an international industrial producer of international commodities. To that end we must do our best to create an amicable atmosphere in international relations. If we have the reputation of liking war or of being militarists, [a policy of] international cooperation will be impossible. We must resolutely follow a policy of peace. It is essential to make all foreigners feel that the Japanese have been converted from their old religion and have become advocates of peace. For that reason we must as far as possible eliminate international barriers. In that sense, a commercial treaty with China is probably necessary. For this same purpose, the abolition of unnecessary tariffs is also required. I wonder if the best way to manage the post-resumption [that is, after Japan's return to the Gold Standard] financial world is not to eliminate the various international barriers, [but] to adopt a viewpoint as similar as possible to that of the foreigner and to maintain close cooperation with foreigners.

The Amau Declaration, 1934

On April 17, 1934, Eiji Amau, official spokesman of Japan's Foreign Ministry, summoned the newspapermen in Tokyo into his office and handed them the following document, in which he claimed that Japan had a special "responsibility for maintenance of peace in East Asia." It furthermore warned other powers against extending loans or other military or political assistance to China. The statement immediately elicited protests from the United States as a violation of the Open Door Policy, which had formed the basis for U.S. policy in China since 1899. According to the Open Door, the United States hoped to keep China open to trade with all powers, with no particular state claiming exclusive rights in any part of the country. In the Nine-Power Pact, signed in Washington, D.C., in 1922, Japan had essentially agreed to live by the terms of the Open Door, promising "to respect the sovereignty, the independence, and the territorial and administrative integrity of China."

SOURCE: *The Amau Declaration, April 1934,* Papers Relating to the Foreign Relations of the United States, Japan, 1931–1941, *vol. I (Washington, DC: U.S. Government Printing Office, 1943).*

UNOFFICIAL STATEMENT BY THE JAPANESE FOREIGN OFFICE, APRIL 17, 1934

Owing to the special position of Japan in her relations with China, her views and attitude respecting matters that concern China, may not agree in every point with those of foreign nations: but it must be realized that Japan is called upon to exert the utmost effort in carrying out her mission and in fulfilling her special responsibilities in East Asia.

Japan has been compelled to withdraw from the League of Nations because of their failure to agree in their opinions on the fundamental principles of preserving peace in East Asia. Although Japan's attitude toward China may at times differ from that of foreign countries, such difference cannot be evaded, owing to Japan's position and mission.

It goes without saying that Japan at all times is endeavouring to maintain and promote her friendly relations with foreign nations, but at the same time we consider it only natural that, to keep peace and order in East Asia, we must even act alone on our own responsibility and it is our duty to perform it. At the same time, there is no country but China which is in a position to share with Japan the responsibility for the maintenance of peace in East Asia. Accordingly, unification of China, preservation of her territorial integrity, as well as restoration of order in that country, are most ardently desired by Japan. History shows that these can be attained through no other means than the awakening and the voluntary efforts of China herself. We oppose therefore any attempt on the part of China to avail herself of the influence of any other country in order to resist Japan: We also oppose any action taken by China, calculated to play one power against another. Any joint operations undertaken by foreign powers even in the name of technical or financial assistance at this particular moment after the Manchurian and Shanghai Incidents are bound to acquire political significance. Undertakings of such nature, if carried through to the end, must give rise to complications that might eventually necessitate discussion of problems like fixing spheres of influence or even international control or division of China, which would be the greatest possible misfortune for China and at the same time would have the most serious repercussion upon Japan and East Asia. Japan therefore must object to such undertakings as a matter of principle, although she will not find it necessary to interfere with any foreign country negotiating individually with China on questions of finance or trade, as long as such negotiations benefit China and are not detrimental to the maintenance of peace in East Asia.

However, supplying China with war planes, building aerodromes in China and detailing military instructors or military advisers to China or contracting a loan to provide funds for political uses, would obviously tend to alienate the friendly relations between Japan and China and other countries and to disturb peace and order in East Asia. Japan will oppose such projects.

The foregoing attitude of Japan should be clear from the policies she has pursued in the past. But, on account of the fact that positive movements for joint action in China by foreign powers under one pretext or another are reported to be on foot, it is deemed not inappropriate to reiterate her policy at this time.

The U.S. Response to the Amau Declaration, 1934

The following is Secretary of State Cordell Hull's summary of a conversation that he had on May 19, 1934, with the Japanese ambassador to the United States.

SOURCE: *U.S. Department of State, Publication 1983*, Peace and War: United States Foreign Policy, 1931–1941 *(Washington, DC: U.S. Government Printing Office, 1943), pp. 223–25.*

I then stated that I had kept perfectly quiet while Japanese officials all the way from Tokyo to Geneva on April 17th [i.e., the Amau Declaration], and for many days following, were reported as giving out to the press the views and policies of the Japanese Government touching certain international phases relating to the Orient; that at the conclusion of these different statements I felt, in order not to be misunderstood here or anywhere, that I should in a respectful and friendly spirit offer a succinct but comprehensive restatement of rights, interests, and obligations as they related to my country primarily and as they related to all countries signatory to the Nine-Power Treaty, the Kellogg Pact, and international law as the same applied to the Orient.

[. . .] I then remarked that I would be entirely frank by saying that just now there was considerable inquiry everywhere as to just why his government singled out the clause or formula about Japan's claiming superior and special interests in the peace situation in "Eastern Asia" and her superior rights or duties in connection with the preservation of peace there; and that many were wondering whether this phrase or formula had ulterior or ultimate implications partaking of the nature of an overlordship of the Orient or a definite purpose to secure preferential trade rights as rapidly as possible in the Orient or "Eastern Asia"—to use the Japanese expression. The Ambassador commenced protesting that this was not the meaning contemplated or intended. I said it would be much simpler and easier if when the national of any other government engaged in some act in the Orient which Japan might reasonably feel would affect her unsatisfactorily, to bring up the individual circumstance to the proper government, instead of issuing a blanket formula which would cause nations everywhere to inquire or surmise whether it did not contemplate an overlordship of the Orient and an attempt at trade preferences as soon as possible. The Ambassador again said that this so-called formula about the superior interests of Japan in preserving peace, etc., did not contemplate the interference or domination or overlordship such as I had referred to.

I stated that to-day there was universal talk and plans about armaments on a steadily increasing scale and that Japan and Germany were the two countries considered chiefly responsible for that talk; that, of course, if the world understood the absence of any overlordship intentions or other unwarranted interference by his government, as the Ambassador stated them to me, his country would not be the occasion for armament discussion in so many parts of the world; and that this illustrated what I had said at the beginning of our conversation that nations should make it a special point to understand each other, and the statesmen of each country should be ready at all times to correct or explain any trouble-making rumors or irresponsible or inaccurate statements calculated to breed distrust and misunderstanding and lukewarmness between nations. I went on to say that it was never so important for the few existing civilized countries of the world to work wholeheartedly together; and that this action of course would, more fully than any other, promote the welfare of the people of each and also would best preserve civilization. I emphasized again that it would be the height of folly for any of the civilized nations to pursue any line of utterances or professed policies that would engender a feeling of unfairness or treaty violation or other unsatisfactory reaction in the important nations who might have both rights and obligations in a given part of the world such as the Orient. I said that in this awful crisis through which the world was passing, debtors everywhere were not keeping faith with creditors in many instances; that sanctity of treaties, in Western Europe especially, was being ignored and violated [Hull is referring here to violations of the Treaty of Versailles by Hitler's government in Germany]; that this was peculiarly a time when our civilized countries should be especially vigilant to observe and to preserve both legal and moral obligations; and that my country especially felt that way, not only on its own account but for the sake of preserving the better and the higher standards of both individual and national conduct everywhere.

I remarked that my Government, apart from its general treaty obligations, was only interested in the equality of trade rights in the Orient as in every part of the world and also its obligations and rights under the law of nations; that what little trade we had in the Orient we naturally desired to conduct on this basis of equality, even though it might be less in the future than now. Then I remarked that if these treaties which imposed special obligations on my government in the Orient were not in existence that, while interested in peace in all parts of the world, my government would also be interested in equality of trade rights.

I inquired whether his government had any disposition to denounce and get rid of these treaties in whole or in part, and said that to ignore or violate them would be embarrassing to my government, and that this would relieve it of any possibilities of such embarrassment. I said that I was not remotely suggesting in the matter. He replied that his government was not disposed to denounce and abrogate these treaties. He said that they felt obliged to get out of the League of Nations on account of certain considerations which their membership created. [. . .]

On the Basic Meaning of National Defense and Its Intensification, 1934

In 1934 the Japanese Army began publishing pamphlets calling for national mobilization for an anticipated future war. This particular pamphlet declared that "war is the father of creation and the mother of culture" and sought to explain to its readers why the waging of future wars would require the creation of a "national defense state" which would organize and direct the entire society's energies toward victory.

SOURCE: *W. Theodore de Bary et al., eds.*, Sources of Japanese Tradition. *Volume Two: 1600–2000.* *Part Two: 1868–2000 (New York: Columbia University Press, 2006), pp. 299–301.*

The essence of national defense policy must be the organization and administration of the nation-state to manifest the highest level of its total energy. [. . .]

The extraordinary development of science and technology and the growing complexity of international relations have invariably widened the scale of war. Armed warfare does not occur in isolation but develops simultaneously with diplomatic warfare, economic warfare, ideological warfare, and other kinds of warfare. Coordinating these elements into war goals and preparing a wartime leadership structure during peacetime have become inextricably linked to the achievement of victory in war.

From these circumstances sprang the idea of total mobilization as the basis for armed conflict, an idea much talked about since the Great War. Total mobilization is the means by which the army and the people unite in a single body to carry on armed warfare. [. . .]

National defense is not aimed just at armed warfare arising from international competition; it is the energy and force behind the life of the nation. The idea that national defense is the actualization of the fundamental energy sustaining the creation and development of the nation-state is absolutely central to the life of the nation. As international rivalry intensifies and international struggle for supremacy spreads, national defense is of the utmost necessity to clarify the ideals of our imperial land and to emerge victorious in the violent competition. [. . .]

To secure the future of our imperial land, we must adopt various necessary emergency measures to overcome the current emergency. It will be difficult, but we must succor the masses who have grown poor under the present system and improve the living standards of the nation's people. We must exert ourselves to achieve the highest level of our national strength by reexamining all our national state organizations in light of our relations with the outside world; by resolutely carrying out a fundamental reconstruction of our national finances, our national economy, our diplomacy, and our education of the people; by organizing and harnessing the enormous latent spiritual strength of our imperial land for the sake of national defense; and by managing all this in a consistent and unified way. These measures will at the same time serve as policies to deal with the crisis now confronting our imperial land.

Some take the optimistic view that international conflict is not inevitable in the present situation and that we can turn things to our advantage solely through diplomatic means. But such are the views of people who do not understand international conditions. [. . .]

We have described the goal and essence of national defense. To summarize, it is the fundamental energy behind the creation and development of the nation-state. Naturally, it is wrong to argue that the scale and content of a country's absolute national defense should be tied to how large or small a country is or how wealthy or poor it is. In this world it is an undeniable axiom that every country has an autonomous and independent right of national defense. It is clear that efforts in the past to limit or prohibit military preparedness by means of international treaties have been little more than subterfuges of the Powers to maintain the superiority of their own national defense under the name of pacifism. No internationalist can deny this fact.

Fundamental Principles of National Policy, 1936

The Hirota Cabinet reported the following to the emperor on August 15, 1936. It would remain the official "blueprint" for Japanese foreign policy until the outbreak of World War II.

SOURCE: *Military History Section, Headquarters, Army Forces Far East, preparer, "Political Strategy Prior to Outbreak of War, Part I, Appendix No. 1,"* in The Japanese Monographs, *available at www .ibiblio.org/pha/monos/index.html.*

1. The aims of our state administration are to stabilize the government at home, and to promote better diplomatic and trade relations abroad. It is in line with the fundamental principles of the Empire that we should seek to become in name and in fact a stabilizing power for assuring peace in East Asia, thereby ultimately contributing to the peace and welfare of humanity. The fundamental national policy for Japan, dictated by the prevailing domestic and international situation, is the securing of a firm diplomatic and defensive position on the East Asiatic Continent and the extension of national influence as far as the South Seas. The following is the outline of the basic program for the realization of these aims:

a. It is the embodiment of the spirit of the Japanese way of life to attempt to achieve unity in East Asia based on a "live-and-let-live" principle. This may be accomplished by destroying the Great Powers' East Asiatic policy of aggression. This should be the principle aim of our foreign policy.

b. National defense will be brought to a level necessary for Japan to secure her position as the stabilizing power in East Asia. This will be accomplished through preservation of her peace and safeguarding her development.

c. Our basic policies for the continent include the elimination of the menace of the Soviet Union by assisting in the sound development of Manchukuo and strengthening the Japan-Manchukuo defense setup, preparing against Great Britain and the United States economic development by bringing about the close cooperation of Manchukuo, Japan and China. In carrying out these policies, care must be exercised to avoid aggravating friendly relations with other nations.

d. In our national and economic expansion to the South Seas, especially to the outer South Seas area, our influence will be extended gradually and by peaceful means, with utmost care being exercised to avoid provoking other nations. This development, together with the healthy growth of Manchukuo, will contribute to the repletion of our national strength.

2. All our domestic and international policies will be adjusted and unified along lines of the basic national policies mentioned above. New administrative policies and actions in conformity with the current situation will be effected, and the following measures; will be taken for this purpose:

a. National defense and armament.

(1) The repletion of Army forces will aim at strength [sufficient] to resist the forces the Soviet Union can employ in the Far East. The garrisons in Manchukuo and Korea will be replenished in order that they can deliver the initial blow to Soviet forces in the Far East at the outbreak of hostilities.

(2) Naval rearmament will be brought to a level sufficient to secure command of the Western Pacific against the United States Navy.

b. Foreign policy will be revamped with a view to achieving our fundamental national policy. The Army and Navy, while avoiding all direct action, will do everything possible to facilitate the working of the diplomatic machinery.

c. In order that the revision of political and administrative structures, the establishment of economic and financial policies, and the operation of all facilities may conform with the fundamental national policy mentioned above, the following measures will be taken:

(1) The people's determination to overcome the crisis will be strengthened by guiding and unifying public opinion.

(2) Administrative structures and economic systems will be reformed with a view to promoting industries essential for the execution of national policy and reviving vitally necessary foreign trade.

(3) Proper measures will be taken to establish good living conditions for the people, increase their bodily strength and foster sound thinking.

(4) Appropriate measures will be taken for the rapid expansion of aviation and shipbuilding industries.

(5) Policies aimed at self-sufficiency in resources and materials essential to national defense and industry will be established.

(6) Diplomatic activities and cultural propaganda abroad will be intensified through the revision of the diplomatic set-up as well as by information and propaganda agencies.

FOREIGN POLICY OF THE EMPIRE

Foreign policy will be based on the accomplishment of our national policy. In order to bring all actions into line with national policy, close liaison will be maintained with all civil and military authorities dispatched abroad. Moreover, positive guidance will be given to the people and complete control will be effected over diplomacy. For the protection and promotion of our just and proper national rights and interests, a self-effacing attitude is to be avoided and a positive one taken. At the same time, efforts will be made to allay the Great Powers' suspicion and apprehension toward the Empire.

I. Over-All Policy

Our fundamental foreign policy aims at the establishment of the Empire as the stabilizing power in East Asia to secure lasting peace in this part of the world and to assure the existence and advancement of the Empire. To this end, the growth of Manchukuo will be promoted, our special and inseparable relations with that country will be further strengthened, our relations with the Soviet Union and China will be independently adjusted from a global standpoint, and our advancement to the South Seas area will be made peacefully. In recent years, the Soviet Union has strengthened sharply its national defense and international positional. It has reinforced its forces in the Far East to an unwarranted degree, exerting increasing military and revolutionary pressure against this region. Moreover, the Soviet Union is planning the communication of all areas of this region, seeking to force the Empire into still more disadvantageous positions. This is a direct menace to the national security of the Empire and a serious obstacle to the execution of current East Asian policy. Therefore, emphasis will be laid for the present on the frustration of Soviet aggressive designs in the Far East. In particular, we should seek through diplomatic means to eliminate the menace of Soviet armament and halt its communization attempt, while working for the replenishment of national defense armament. Accordingly, it is necessary that the Empire, considering the over-all current international situation, adjust her relations with major powers, and bring her diplomatic machinery into operation, thereby making the situation more favorable to us.

II. Outline of the Program

1. In view of the current domestic and international situation, extreme caution will be exercised to avoid causing trouble with the Soviet Union, and efforts will be exerted to settle problems entirely by peaceful means.

a. Commissions will be established to decide the frontier line extending from the Khanda Lake to the Tumen River and to arbitrate on frontier zone conflicts. Similar functioning bodies will be created for the Manchukuo-Soviet and Manchukuo-Mongolian borders.

b. At an appropriate time a proposal will be made for the establishment of a demilitarized zone.

c. In the event the Soviet Union expresses a desire to conclude a non-aggression pact, the Empire will clearly signify its intention of agreeing, on the condition that both countries set the problems, including the problem of adjusting their military forces in the Far East, to bring about a balance of power.

d. Appropriate measures will be taken to prevent the Soviet Union from committing ideological infiltration into Japan, Manchukuo and China.

2. A dignified attitude and just measures will be adopted in dealing with Chinese central and local governments. Coupled with our economic measures for the Chinese masses, steps will be taken to guarantee correction of their attitude toward Japan. Thus, friendly cooperation between the two countries, based on the "live-and-let-live" principle, will surely materialize. In the North China area, measures will be taken to realize economic and cultural cooperation with Japan and Manchukuo, and efforts will be made to turn North China into a special area where Japan, Manchukuo and China will join in mutual defense against communistic inroads from the Soviet Union. As regard local governments, other than that of North China, measures will not be taken to either further or obstruct the unification or split of China.

The above are the basic principles of our China policy, upon which all our practical measures will be based. In view of our present relationship with the Soviet Union, priority will be given in forming our China policy to making North China a special anti-Communist, pro-Japanese and pro-Manchukuo area, obtaining resources for our national defense program, and the expansion of communication facilities. (Plans requiring immediate execution will be dealt with separately.)

3. The improvement of friendly relations between our country and the United States might greatly contribute to offsetting British and Soviet influences. However, in view of the fact that the United States is engaged in rearming and views the development of our China policy with great concern in the light of her traditional Far Eastern policy, there is the danger that she may assist China, making that country dependent on the West. Moreover, it is feared that this would eventually create a situation exceedingly unfavorable to the execution of our policy against the Soviet Union. Therefore, we must seek the United States' understanding of our just attitude through respect for her commercial interests in China. At the same time, we should endeavor to improve friendly relations based on economic interdependence, thereby causing the United States to refrain from interfering with our Far Eastern policy.

4. Since the development of the political situation in Europe has an important bearing on East Asia, efforts must be exerted to turn it to our advantage, particularly to hold the Soviet Union in check.

a. Great Britain and Japan have many areas of conflicting interests. In view of the fact that Great Britain, among the western powers, has the greatest stake in the Far East and since the attitude of other European countries depends largely upon that of Great Britain, it is especially important for us to take the initiative at this time to improve relations with Great Britain. In this way Great Britain may side with us in our relations with the Soviet Union and act as a counterbalance against the Soviets, thereby lessening the obstacles lying in the way of our overseas expansion. Since the adjustment of Anglo-Japanese relations in China will have far-reaching results, we must endeavor to take appropriate measures for breaking the deadlock over China and for making an over-all adjustment in Anglo-Japanese relations. This is to be accomplished through efforts to get Great Britain to recognize and respect Japan's special and vital interest, especially in China, and also through respecting Great Britain's rights and interests there. We must, nevertheless, guard against Great Britain, lest she adopt a policy of applying pressure against Japan in concert with other powers, particularly the United States, the Soviet Union and China.

b. Germany, in her relations with the Soviet Union, is in much the same position as Japan. In view of the special relationship between France and the Soviet Union, it is deemed advantageous for Germany to act in concert with Japan in matters of national defense and anti-Communist policy. Therefore, our friendly relations with Germany are to be improved and measures are to be taken to realize Japanese-German collaboration as occasion demands. Moreover, this relationship is to be expanded to include such countries as Poland, with a view to checking the Soviet Union. In addition, efforts are to be made to enlighten Moslem [sic] nations and European and Asian countries neighboring the Soviet Union, with attention paid to the improvement of friendly relations with those nations.

5. Occupying an important position in our global trade relations and being an area indispensable for the industrial and national defense of the Empire, as well as a natural field for our racial development, the Southern Region mist be studied as an area for our expansion. But our advance in that area must be conducted peacefully and gradually, with utmost efforts exerted to prevent provocation of other countries and to allay their misgivings against the Empire.

As for the Philippines, we will look forward to her complete independence and, if called upon, be ready to guarantee her neutrality.

For our expansion into the Netherlands East Indies, it is extremely important that we allay the misgivings of the people toward us and convert them into a pro-Japanese nation. Appropriate measures, therefore, will be taken for this purpose. If need be a non-aggression pact with Holland will be concluded.

Thailand and other underdeveloped nations should be given proper guidance and assistance on the basis of our principle of coexistence and coprosperity.

6. Overseas trade is not only indispensable for the maintenance and betterment of the economic life of our nation but also contributes to the improvement of our finances and the state of our international obligations. It is particularly important, under the current domestic and international situation, that foreign trade be expanded to the utmost. Thus, we must develop our economic power by rationalizing our foreign trade and at the same time acquiring important natural resources through proper adjustment of our interests to those of other powers.

The U.S. Response to the Outbreak of War between China and Japan, 1937

In response to the outbreak of fighting between Chinese and Japanese forces near Beijing, U.S. Secretary of State Cordell Hull on July 16, 1937, laid out the principles that would guide U.S. policy toward East Asia over the next four years. Hull's habit of speaking in generalities rather than addressing specific cases (note, for example, that he mentions neither Japan nor China by name) was an ongoing source of frustration in Tokyo.

SOURCE: Peace and War: United States Foreign Policy, 1931–1941 *(Washington, DC: U.S. Government Printing Office, 1943), pp. 370–71.*

I have been receiving from many sources inquiries and suggestions arising out of disturbed situations in various parts of the world.

Unquestionably there are in a number of regions tensions and strains which on their face involve only countries that are near neighbors but which in ultimate analysis are of inevitable concern to the whole world. Any situation in which armed hostilities are in progress or are threatened is a situation wherein rights and interests of all nations either are or may be seriously affected. There can be no serious hostilities anywhere in the world which will not one way or another affect interests or rights or obligations of this country. I therefore feel warranted in making—in fact, I feel it a duty to make—a statement of this Government's position in regard to international problems and situations with respect to which this country feels deep concern.

This country constantly and consistently advocates maintenance of peace. We advocate national and international self-restraint. We advocate abstinence by all nations from use of force in pursuit of policy and from interference in the internal affairs of other nations. We advocate adjustment of problems in international relations by processes of peaceful negotiation and agreement. We advocate faithful observance of international agreements. Upholding the principle of the sanctity of treaties, we believe in modification of provisions of treaties when need therefore arises, by orderly processes carried out in a spirit of mutual helpfulness and accommodation. We believe in respect by all nations for the rights of others and performance by all nations of established obligations. We stand for revitalizing and strengthening of international law. We advocate steps toward promotion of economic security and stability the world over. We advocate lowering or removing of excessive barriers in international trade. We seek effective equality of commercial opportunity and we urge upon all nations application of the principle of equality of treatment. We believe in limitation and reduction of armament. Realizing the necessity for maintaining armed forces adequate for national security, we are prepared to reduce or to increase our own armed forces in proportion to reductions or increases made by other countries. We avoid entering into alliances or entangling commitments but we believe in cooperative effort by peaceful and practicable means in support of the principles hereinbefore stated.

KONOE FUMIMARO

On Japan's Goals in China, 1938

Born into Japan's ancient Fujiwara clan, Konoe Fumimaro became a prince of the empire at the age of twelve, when his father died. He studied economics at Kyoto Imperial University and was invited to participate in the Paris Peace Conference as part of the Japanese delegation. Before attending, however, he wrote an essay titled "Reject the Anglo-American-Centered Peace," which won him the acclaim of Pan-Asianists. As a member of the House of Peers he won popular acclaim for supporting a bill that gave suffrage to all Japanese men twenty-five years or older, and in 1933 he was elected president of the House of Peers. Four years later he became prime minister for the first time, but only a month after he took office fighting broke out between Chinese and Japanese troops just outside Beijing. Konoe authorized the dispatch of reinforcements but instructed the army not to escalate the fighting. The generals ignored this order, leading to what quickly became known as the "China Incident."

In December 1938, with no end in sight to the conflict that had begun nearly eighteen months earlier, Konoe issued a public statement regarding Japan's reasons for keeping up the fight. His call for a "new order in East Asia" would later be expanded to the much clunkier "Greater East Asia Co-Prosperity Sphere."

SOURCE: *Statement by the Japanese Prime Minister (Prince Konoye), December 22, 1938;* Papers Relating to the Foreign Relations of the United States, Japan, 1931–1941, vol. I (Washington, DC: U.S. Government Printing Office, 1943).

The Japanese Government is resolved, as has been clearly set forth in its two previous statements issued this year, to carry on the military operations for the complete extermination of the anti-Japanese Kuomintang Government, and at the same time to proceed with the work of establishing a new order in East Asia together with those far-sighted Chinese who share in our ideals and aspirations.

The spirit of renaissance is now sweeping over all parts of China and enthusiasm for reconstruction is mounting ever higher. The Japanese Government desires to make public its basic policy for adjusting relations between Japan and China, in order that its intentions may be thoroughly understood both at home and abroad.

Japan, China and Manchukuo will be united by the common aim of establishing the new order in East Asia and of realizing a relationship of neighborly amity, common defense against Communism and economic cooperation. For that purpose it is necessary first of all that China should cast aside all narrow and prejudiced views belonging to the past and do away with the folly of anti-Japanism and resentment regarding Manchukuo. In other words, Japan frankly desires China to enter of her own will into complete diplomatic relations with Manchukuo.

The existence of the Comintern influence in East Asia cannot be tolerated. Japan therefore considers it an essential condition of the adjustment of the Sino-Japanese relations that there should be concluded an anti-Comintern agreement between the two countries in consonance with the spirit of the anti-Comintern agreement between Japan, Germany and Italy. And, in order to insure the full accomplishment of her purpose, Japan demands, in view of the actual circumstances prevailing in China, that Japanese troops be stationed, as an anti-Communist measure, at specified points during the time the said agreement is in force, and also that the Inner Mongolian region be designated as a special anti-Communist area.

As regards economic relations between the two countries, Japan does not intend to exercise economic monopoly in China, nor does she intend to demand of China to limit the interests of those third Powers who grasp the meaning of the new East Asia and are willing to act accordingly. Japan only seeks to render effective the cooperation and collaboration between the two countries. That is to say, Japan demands that China, in accordance with the principle of equality between the two countries, should recognize the freedom of residence and trade on the part of Japanese subjects in the interior of China, with a view to promoting the economic interests of both peoples; and that, in the light of the historical and economic relations between the two nations, China should extend to Japan facilities for the development of China's natural resources, especially in the regions of North China and Inner Mongolia.

The above gives the general lines of what Japan demands of China.

If the true object of Japan in conducting the present vast military campaign be fully understood, it will be plain that what she seeks is neither territory nor indemnity for the costs of military operations. Japan demands only the minimum guaranty needed for the execution by China of her function as a participant in the establishment of the new order.

Japan not only respects the sovereignty of China, but she is prepared to give positive consideration to the questions of the abolition of extraterritoriality and of the rendition of concessions and settlements matters which are necessary for the full independence of China.

RYŪ SHINTARŌ

From Japan's Economic Reorganization, 1940

Ryū Shintarō, a journalist and close adviser to Prime Minister Konoe, first published his call for a planned economy in the influential literary magazine Chūō kōron in 1939, then expanded it into a full-length book the following year. It quickly became a best seller, although members of the business community regarded Ryū's views as tantamount to Communism. In the following excerpt the author argues for strict controls on profits and for separating management of a firm from ownership of it.

SOURCE: *W. Theodore de Bary et al., eds.*, Sources of Japanese Tradition, *Volume Two: 1600–2000, Part Two: 1868–2000 (New York: Columbia University Press, 2006), pp. 305–08.*

INVESTMENT AND CONTROLS ON THE PROFIT RATE

Investors of capital argue that if profits are placed under government control, productive activities will stagnate. [. . .] Others object [to government controls on company profits] on the fundamental economic ground that according to the tenets of liberalism the source of all productive activity lies in the human impulse toward "gain." This view dominates the conventional wisdom of today's businessmen.

With respect to the first point [. . .] the fear the production will stagnate] is an illusion that results from the concentration of capital in the high-profit sector. The high-profit sector invigorates and stimulates productive activity, but it does so only relatively compared with other sectors. If the present dividend rate were to continue fluctuating at around 30 percent, would investment slow down if dividends were held under 30 percent? [. . .]

THE PURSUIT OF GAIN

Let us turn to the second point. This is the problem of *Homo economicus* (economic man) familiar to every first-year economics student wrestling with Adam Smith. In these final days of liberalism, it is probably inevitable that we must mention Smith, the founding father of liberalism.

The essence of liberalism lies in the proposition that when individuals pursue their own gain as they compete with one another to express their distinctive characteristics, they are acting in complete accord with the public good. Basically, this proposition rests on the assumption that an individual's "creativity" or "originality" derives from his "pursuit of gain" and that without pursuing one's gains, it is not possible to display one's creativity or originality.

This way of thinking lies at the core of economic liberalism. Transcending this way of thinking must be the point of departure for building a new economic system. [. . .]

[. . .] In a liberal economy "pursuit of gain" must be tolerated, but in itself it is nothing more than the economic psychology of those who find themselves in an economy organized on liberal principles. [. . .]

THE MOTIVE FOR ACTION IN MODERN BUSINESS FIRMS

Since the modern business firm is organized for the continual pursuit of profit, what is at issue here is clearly not a question of human nature but a question of economic organization. It is safe to say that even systems based on liberal [economic] principles are, for the most part, moving in the direction of "functionality."

Looked at in this way, the idea that controls on profits will slow down productive activity or bring the economy to a halt is behind the times. It reflects the mentality of a small shopkeeper who thinks the commercial spirit of the greengrocer or the fishmonger is what drives the modern business firm. The problem clearly is to free the development of productive power by stripping the old shell from modern business firms that have developed on the basis of functional specialization, by emphasizing their "functional" position and by transforming them from "organizations based on profit to "organizations based on function."

THE CONTROL OF PROFITS AND THE FREEDOM OF CREATIVITY

However, since an organization based on function constitutes a unified whole, we must decisively regulate profits, which are at the core of a liberal economic system.

The control of profits involves both a reduction and a fixing of the dividend rate. What the system must determine is not how high the dividend rate should be but, rather, how upper limits on the dividend rate can be fixed at a level appropriate to current conditions. Since we can imagine that at some point there will be an economic turndown, it ought to be set at a low level [. . .] the point of departure for the new system lies in whether or not dividends should be considered equivalent to interest payments. More specifically, since profits over and above the fixed dividend are either retained as company reserves or used directly in the expansion of the business firm, not only must profits be considered as interest payments but the meaning of invested capital also must change to some degree. Since the owners of capital simply collect fixed dividends similar to a kind of interest payment, the function of the businessman and the position of the capitalist differ. There is no reason why a capitalist cannot also be a businessman at the same time, of course, but his function [in each role] is quite distinct. The businessman assumes the role of a purely managerial technician charged with running the business firm. He sees to it that the company pays fixed dividends on capital, but beyond that he has no responsibility toward the capitalist. On the other hand, as a business manager, he has an enormous responsibility toward the state and society. His function is to manage the enterprise in its state and social roles with the highest degree of efficiency, and it is for that that he is rewarded.

Just as the engineer carries out his state and social functions through his technical contributions, [. . .] so too the businessman [in his role as manager] acts like an "engineer" for a particular business firm. In that sense he stands as a true leader of production. Since he is completely liberated from the supervision of the capitalist, he acquires freedom of "creativity" in running the business firm. His "creativity" is not driven by moneymaking, as it once was. As he becomes conscious of his role in society, he achieves a new and purer freedom. Today both the businessman and the capitalist must put aside the notion that profit is everything, or to put it another way, a framework based on individualistic economic activity. By carrying out their own particular "function" in state and society. If they act individualistically by putting profit ahead of everything else, businessmen will gradually lose their "public voice." [. . .] Only by putting aside their individualism and their profit seeking will their public views acquire political weight. In the view of the current political situation facing Japan, it is extraordinarily important that they do so.

DRAFT TREATIES

Neither of the two historical treaties in this section was concluded before July 1940 and are thus not in effect at the start of the game. They are included in the game book as suggested language for treaties that might be negotiated with foreign powers in the game.

SOURCE FOR BOTH SELECTIONS: *Military History Section, Headquarters, Army Forces Far East, preparer,* Political Strategy Prior to Outbreak of War, Part II, *available at http://ibiblio.org/pha /monos/146/index.html.*

Draft of the Tripartite Pact

The governments of Germany, Italy and Japan, considering it as a condition precedent of any lasting peace that all nations of the world be given each its own proper place, have decided to stand by and co-operate with one another in regard to their efforts in greater East Asia and regions of Europe respectively wherein it is their prime purpose to establish and maintain a new order of things calculated to promote the mutual prosperity and welfare of the peoples concerned.

Furthermore, it is the desire of the three governments to extend co-operation to such nations in other spheres of the world as may be inclined to put forth endeavours along lines similar to their own, in order that their ultimate aspirations for world peace may thus be realized.

Accordingly, the governments of Germany, Italy and Japan have agreed as follows:

Article ONE: Japan recognizes and respects the leadership of Germany and Italy in establishment of a new order in Europe.

Article TWO: Germany and Italy recognize and respect the leadership of Japan in the establishment of a new order in greater East Asia.

Article THREE: Germany, Italy and Japan agree to co-operate in their efforts on aforesaid lines. They further undertake to assist one another with all political, economic and military means when one of the three contracting powers is attacked by a power at present not involved in the European war or in the Chinese-Japanese conflict.

Article FOUR: With the view to implementing the present pact, joint technical commissions, members which are to be appointed by the respective governments of Germany, Italy and Japan will meet without delay.

Article FIVE: The present pact shall come into effect immediately upon signature and shall remain in force 10 years from the date of its coming into force. At the proper time before expiration of said term, the high contracting parties shall at the request of any of them enter into negotiations for its renewal.[1]

In faith whereof, the undersigned duly authorized by their respective governments have signed this pact and have affixed hereto their signatures.

---

1. *In the final version of the treaty, Article Five was a clause specifically exempting the signatories from any obligation to go to war against the Soviet Union. The text listed here under Article Five became Article Six.*

The Fundamental Principles for the Readjustment of Relations between Japan and China, 1940

This document, approved by the cabinet in January 1940, embodies Japan's main demands from China. The provision for continued Japanese occupation of north China and Mongolia, and the demand that China recognize the "independent" status of Manchukuo, were both unacceptable to Jiang Jieshi.

Japan, Manchukuo and China will unite as good neighbors in mutual support of each other with the ultimate goal of establishing a new order in East Asia and will seek, as their common objective, the creation of an axis for peace in the Orient. The fundamental principles to be realized are:

1. Principles for cooperation between Japan, Manchukuo and China based on reciprocity, a good neighbor policy, and joint anti-Comintern and economic coalition principles, will be established.

2. Zones in which close cooperation between Japan and China for national defense and economic reasons will be practiced, will be established in North China and Mongolia. In addition, in Mongolia special military and administrative positions for anti-Comintern defense will be established.

3. In the area along the lower reaches of the Yangtze River, close economic cooperation will be effected between Japan and China.

4. Close military cooperation in the specially designated islands off the coast of South China (Hainan Island and Quemoy Island off Amoy) will be effected.

5. In order to achieve this an agreement will be concluded in with "The Specific Principles for the Readjustment of Relations between Japan and China."

The Specific Principles for the Readjustment of Relations between Japan and China.

I. GOOD NEIGHBOR POLICY

Japan, Manchukuo and China will respect each other's inherent characteristics, cooperate closely to secure peace in the Orient, conceive measures for mutual aid and amity in various fields in order to fulfill a good neighbor policy.

a. China will recognize Manchukuo. Japan will respect the integrity of the territories and the administration and sovereignty of China. Japan, Manchukuo and China will resume new friendly relations.

b. Japan, Manchukuo, and China will remove any measures or cause which might destroy friendship in the various fields of politics, diplomacy, education, propaganda and trade, and will prohibit their introduction in the future.

c. Japan, Manchukuo and China will conduct diplomatic relations based on mutual cooperation.

d. Japan, Manchukuo and China will cooperate in the creation, blending and development of culture.

e. As friendly relations between Japan, Manchukuo and China are restored, Japan will gradually consider the return of concessions and extraterritorial rights.

II. JOINT ANTI-COMINTERN DEFENSE

Manchukuo and China will enter into a joint anti-Comintern defense pact.

a. Japan, Manchukuo and China will eradicate communistic elements and organizations in their territories, and will cooperate with each other relative to information and propaganda concerning anti-Comintern defense.

b. Japan and China will jointly carry out anti-Comintern defense. To this end, Japan will station troops in areas deemed necessary.

c. Japan and China will cooperate with each other in the preservation of public order.

d. China will, under separate agreement, comply with the requests of Japan, made out of military necessity, on those matters pertinent to garrison areas and on railways, aviation, communications, principal ports and waterways connected therewith. In peacetime, however, Japan will respect the administrative authority and control of China.

III. ECONOMIC COOPERATION

To realize the benefits of mutual aid and anti-Comintern defense, Japan, Manchukuo and China will in essence be equal and reciprocal with a view to offset merits and demerits and minister to each other's wants with respect to industry and economy.

a. In regard to specific resources in North China and Mongolia, especially ore deposits necessary to national defense, Japan and China will cooperate in their exploitation to effect joint anti-Comintern defense and economic cooperation, and in regard to their utilization, special concessions will be granted to Japan upon due consideration of the requests of China.

In other areas, also, necessary concessions will be granted to Japan with respect to exploitation and utilization of specific resources necessary to national defense. In utilizing the resources, the requests of China will be given due consideration.

b. As for industries in general, Japan will render necessary aid to China in accordance with the agreement concluded with the latter.

c. In regard to finance, banking (particularly the establishment of the new Central Bank and circulation of new currency) and the establishment of the economic policy of China, Japan will render the necessary aid to China in accordance with the agreement concluded with the latter.

d. Promotion of commerce and trade between Japan, Manchukuo and China will be developed by respecting tariff autonomy and mutual interest and by the adoption of sound tariff and customs procedures. At the same time, the supply and demand of materials between Japan, Manchukuo and China, especially between North China and Central China, will be facilitated and rationalized insofar as the self-sustenance of each country is maintained.

e. For the development of transportation, communications, meteorology and survey in China, Japan will render the necessary aid to and cooperate with China in accordance with the agreement concluded with the latter.

f. For the construction of a new Shanghai Municipality, Japan will render the necessary aid and cooperation based on the agreement with China.

IV. OTHERS

a. China will, under separate agreement, employ Japanese advisers and staff in charge of matters relative to cooperation between Japan and China.

b. Japan will cooperate in the relief of Chinese destitutes arising out of the Incident.

c. China will indemnify the loss of rights and interests sustained by the Japanese people in China since the outbreak of the Incident.

APPENDIX A

IMPORTANT LOCATIONS

The following locations are all explicitly mentioned in the game. The coordinates refer to the map of East Asia and the Pacific found on p. 16.

Burma (A2, now called Myanmar): Since 1885 the British have controlled Burma. It is largely undeveloped economically but is a fairly rich source of lumber and rubber. Most important, it is the start of the so-called Burma Road, a critical route for Western aid to China. Given Great Britain's troubles in Europe, the British have not been able to station large numbers of troops in the area, so it remains vulnerable to a Japanese attack.

China (A2–B2): The world's most populous country, the Republic of China has been at war with Japan since 1937. The area shaded in dark gray is occupied by Japanese forces, which currently number more than a million men. This area includes the republic's original capital, Nanjing, so the government of Jiang Jieshi is currently based farther west, in Chongqing. Japan seeks a Pan-Asian partnership with China in which Japan receives extensive economic privileges in the country plus the right to station troops indefinitely in its northern provinces. Jiang has up to this point refused to consider Japanese demands and has been receiving aid from the Soviet Union and the West. In the occupied part of China a new government has formed under the leadership of Wang Jingwei, a former political ally of Jiang, but as of July 1940 Japan has yet to recognize the Wang regime officially.

Dutch East Indies (A3–B3, northwest of Australia; main islands are Borneo, Java, and Sumatra, now called Indonesia): A treasure trove of natural resources, most notably oil, these islands have long been the subject of attention from Japan. The government at Jakarta currently supplies no more than a small fraction of Japan's annual petroleum needs. Given that the Netherlands is currently under German occupation, it is unlikely that the islands would be capable of resisting a Japanese attack. The Dutch do, however, maintain a small naval force in the islands that includes three cruisers, seven destroyers, and fifteen submarines.

Formosa (B2, now called Taiwan): The seventh-largest sugar producer in the world, Formosa has been part of the Japanese Empire since 1895, when it was conquered by Japanese forces in the Sino-Japanese War. Since 1935 Tokyo has been conducting an active campaign of assimilation in order to encourage the people of the island to view themselves as Japanese. While this campaign has had only limited success, the island remains critically important to Japan's war effort and is home to a number of military bases and industrial centers.

French Indochina (A2–A3, now divided into Vietnam, Laos, and Kampuchea): The French have had a presence in this region since the 1860s, but in 1887 they consolidated several of these into what they called Indochina. They added more territory in the 1890s and 1900s in a series of victorious wars against neighboring Thailand. Indochina is the source of several strategic raw materials, the most important of which is rubber. It has also been used as a route for Western aid to Jiang Jieshi's regime. Given that France has been overrun by German troops, no more than 50,000 troops are currently stationed in Indochina, making it unlikely that it could be adequately defended against a Japanese attack.

Japan (B2–C2): Japan consists of the four "home islands"—Hokkaido, Honshu, Shikoku, and Kyushu. Yokosuka Naval Base is the home to Japan's Combined Fleet, consisting of ten battleships, seven aircraft carriers, forty cruisers, 109 destroyers, and sixty-three submarines.

Korea (B2, today divided between North and South Korea): Korea was occupied by Japanese troops in 1905, and five years later it was formally annexed to the Japanese Empire. Still, Japanese control has never been popular among the Koreans, who repeatedly staged anti-Japanese rallies in the 1920s. The occupiers responded brutally to these, killing thousands of protesters. With the occupation of Manchuria, however, such protests have died down, since it has become virtually impossible for anti-Japanese forces to receive aid from China or the Soviet Union. As a result, only a small garrison of third-rate troops holds the country.

Malaya (A3, today called Malaysia): The British originally established a presence on the Malay Peninsula in the late eighteenth century, and in 1895 they organized their possessions in the region into the Federated Malay States. Malaya is very lightly defended; however, at the southern tip of the peninsula is Singapore, sometimes called the "Gibraltar of the East" and widely regarded as the most formidable fortress in all of East Asia.

Manchukuo (B1–B2): Formerly part of China, Manchuria was occupied by Japanese troops in 1931 and in the following year was declared to be the "independent" state of Manchukuo under the leadership of Pu-Yi, the former emperor of China. However, it is widely known that the Japanese army is the real power in Manchukuo. Some 700,000 Japanese troops are stationed in the area for possible use against either China or the Soviet Union.

Pearl Harbor (D2): Since spring 1940 Pearl Harbor, on the Hawaiian island of Oahu, has been the home of the U.S. Pacific Fleet. This fleet is the only naval force in the region that poses a serious threat to the Japanese navy and consists of eight battleships, three aircraft carriers, twenty-one cruisers, sixty-seven destroyers, and twenty-seven submarines.

Philippine Islands (B3): The United States captured the Philippine Islands from Spain in 1898, but in 1935 the U.S. Congress voted to grant the islands autonomy, with independence to follow. In the meantime, U.S. forces occupy the Philippines, helping train a Filipino army. The Philippines are also currently the base for the U.S. Asiatic Fleet, consisting of three cruisers, thirteen destroyers, and twenty-nine submarines.

Sakhalin Island (C1): Ever since the end of the Russo-Japanese War of 1904–05 control of this large island has been divided, with the Russians holding the north and the Japanese the south. It has ever since been a bone of contention between the two countries, both of which seek sole control. Sakhalin is sparsely populated—a function of the harsh climate—and possesses very little in the way of resources. The exception is oil; it is estimated that large reserves are available under the frozen, rocky soil. Any effort to extract this oil, however, will encounter significant difficulties. It does not, therefore, offer a short-term solution to Japan's lack of petroleum.

Singapore (A3): At the extreme southern tip of the Malay Peninsula is Singapore, sometimes called the "Gibraltar of the East" and widely regarded as the most formidable fortress in all of East Asia. It is home to a large garrison of British troops, and its massive naval guns make it virtually impregnable to attack from the sea. Moreover, Singapore is the primary naval base in the region for the Royal Navy. Given the situation in Europe, however, no more than twenty or so British and Commonwealth (Australia and New Zealand) warships are stationed there, none of which is a capital ship (that is, a battleship or aircraft carrier).

Thailand (A3): Thailand remains the only part of mainland Asia to have never been colonized by a European power, and the current ruler, King Prajadhipok, has every intention of keeping it that way. Thai foreign policy has tended to be pro-British, but Prajadhipok is known to desire the return of certain territories to the east that were lost to French Indochina after a disastrous war around the turn of the century. Now that France has been overrun by German troops Thailand finally has an opportunity for revenge.

The Soviet Union or **Union of Soviet Socialist Republics (USSR)** (A1–D1, now called Russia): Formerly the Russian Empire, the USSR is currently the world's only communist country and is under the rule of Joseph Stalin. Japan has long coveted its eastern Maritime Province, which lies directly east of Manchukuo. Not only would this extend Manchukuo's territory to the sea, but it would give the country Vladivostok, one of the best natural harbors on the north Pacific. Tokyo also fears that the Soviets are working to spread Communism into East Asia, particularly China. For this reason, there was much talk in the 1930s about going to war against the USSR, but such talk has cooled considerably after the Japanese army suffered an embarrassing defeat at the hands of the Red Army at Nomonhan in 1939. Indeed, since Nomonhan the Soviets have stationed even more troops in the region, so that in 1940 there are no fewer than thirty divisions and some 2,800 aircraft just beyond Manchukuo's northern borders.

APPENDIX B

COMPARATIVE STRENGTHS OF JAPANESE AND U.S. ARMED FORCES IN LATE 1941

	Japan	United States (Pacific Theater)*	United States (Total)
Military Personnel	approx. 2.4 million	approx. 70,000	approx. 1.6 million
Aircraft	2,225	516	4,002
Aircraft Carriers	10	3	8
Battleships	10	9	17
Cruisers	36	22	36
Destroyers	113	63	171
Submarines	63	62	112

*Includes all U.S. forces based at Hawaii, the Philippines, Wake Island, Guam, and Midway.

SOURCE: John Ellis, World War II: The Encyclopedia of Facts and Figures (New York: Military Book Club, 1993).

APPENDIX C

BIBLIOGRAPHY

Players looking for deeper insights regarding their characters or of Japan during this critical era may wish to consult any of the following secondary sources.

Army

Akira, Fujiwara. "The Role of the Japanese Army." In Dorothy Borg and Shumpei Okamoto, eds. *Pearl Harbor as History: Japanese-American Relations, 1931–1941.* New York: Columbia University Press, 1973, pp. 189–95.

Drea, Edward J. *Japan's Imperial Army: Its Rise and Fall.* Lawrence: University Press of Kansas, 2009.

Friday, Karl F. "Bushido or Bull? A Medieval Historian's Perspective on the Imperial Army and the Japanese Warrior Tradition." *The History Teacher* 27.3 (May 1994): 339–49.

Harries, Meirion and Susie Harries. *Soldiers of the Sun: The Rise and Fall of the Imperial Japanese Army.* New York: Random House, 1992.

Bureaucracy

Johnson, Chalmers. *MITI and the Japanese Miracle: The Growth of Industrial Policy, 1925–1975.* Stanford, CA: Stanford University Press, 1982, chap. 4.

Katsumi, Usui. "The Role of the Foreign Ministry." In Dorothy Borg and Shumpei Okamoto, eds. *Pearl Harbor as History: Japanese-American Relations, 1931–1941.* New York: Columbia University Press, 1973, pp. 127–48.

Kerde, Ortrud. "The Ideological Background of the Japanese War Economy: Visions of the 'Reformist Bureaucrats.' " In Erich Pauer, ed. *Japan's War Economy.* London: Routledge, 1999, pp. 23–38.

Spaulding, Robert M. Jr. "Japan's 'New Bureaucrats,' 1932–45." In George M. Wilson, ed. *Crisis Politics in Prewar Japan: Institutional and Ideological Problems of the 1930s.* Tokyo: Sophia University Press, 1970, pp. 51–70.

Takafusa, Nakamura. "The Japanese War Economy as a 'Planned Economy.' " In Erich Pauer, ed. *Japan's War Economy.* London: Routledge, 1999, pp. 9–22.

Imperial Court

Titus, David Anson. *Palace and Politics in Prewar Japan.* New York: Columbia University Press, 1974.

Navy

Hatano, Sumio. "The Japanese Navy and the Development of Southward Expansion." In Shinya Sugiyama and Milagros C. Guerrero, eds. *International Commercial Rivalry in Southeast Asia in the Interwar Period*. New Haven, CT: Yale Southeast Asia Studies, 1994, pp. 95–108.

Jun, Tsunoda. "The Navy's Role in the Southern Strategy." In James William Morley, ed. *The Fateful Choice: Japan's Advance into Southeast Asia, 1939–1941*. New York: Columbia University Press, 1980, pp. 241–95.

Mauch, Peter. "A Bolt from the Blue? New Evidence on the Japanese Navy and the Draft Understanding between Japan and the United States, April 1941." *Pacific Historical Review* 78.1 (2009): 55–79.

Parillo, Mark P. "The Imperial Japanese Navy in World War II." In James J. Sadkovich, ed. *Reevaluating Major Naval Combatants of World War II*. Westport, CT: Greenwood Press, 1990, pp. 61–77.

Sadao, Asada. *From Mahan to Pearl Harbor: The Imperial Japanese Navy and the United States*. Annapolis, MD: U.S. Naval Institute Press, 2006.

———. "The Japanese Navy and the United States." In Dorothy Borg and Shumpei Okamoto, eds. *Pearl Harbor as History: Japanese-American Relations, 1931–1941*. New York: Columbia University Press, 1973, pp. 225–59.

Zaibatsu

Fletcher, William Miles. *The Japanese Business Community and National Trade Policy, 1920–1942*. Chapel Hill: University of North Carolina Press, 1989.

Hajime, Shimizu. "Japanese Economic Penetration into Southeast Asia and the 'Southward Expansion' School of Thought." In Shinya Sugiyama and Milagros C. Guerrero, eds. *International Commercial Rivalry in Southeast Asia in the Interwar Period*. New Haven, CT: Yale Southeast Asia Studies, 1994, pp. 11–39.

Hideichirō, Nakamura. "The Activities of the Japan Economic Federation." In Dorothy Borg and Shumpei Okamoto, eds. *Pearl Harbor as History: Japanese-American Relations, 1931–1941*. New York: Columbia University Press, 1973, pp. 411–20.

Johnson, Chalmers. *MITI and the Japanese Miracle: The Growth of Industrial Policy, 1925–1975*. Stanford, CT: Stanford University Press, 1982, chap. 4.

Katsurō, Yamamura. "The Role of the Finance Ministry." In Dorothy Borg and Shumpei Okamoto, eds. *Pearl Harbor as History: Japanese-American Relations, 1931–1941*. New York: Columbia University Press, 1973, pp. 287–302.

Takafusa, Nakamura. "The Japanese War Economy as a 'Planned Economy.'" In Erich Pauer, ed. *Japan's War Economy*. London: Routledge, 1999, pp. 9–22.

Tiedemann, Arthur E. "Big Business and Politics in Prewar Japan." In James William Morley, ed. *Dilemmas of Growth in Prewar Japan*. Princeton, NJ: Princeton University Press, 1971, pp. 267–316.

Ultranationalists

Skya, Walter. *Japan's Holy War: The Ideology of Radical Shintō Ultranationalism.* Durham, NC: Duke University Press, 2009.

Storry, Richard. *The Double Patriots: A Study of Japanese Nationalism.* London: Chatto & Windus, 1957.

Takashi, Itō. "The Role of Right-Wing Organizations in Japan." In Dorothy Borg and Shumpei Okamoto, eds. *Pearl Harbor as History: Japanese-American Relations, 1931–1941.* New York: Columbia University Press, 1973, pp. 487–509.

Other Works

Barnhart, Michael A. *Japan Prepares for Total War: The Search for Economic Security, 1919–1941.* Ithaca, NY: Cornell University Press, 1987.

Chihiro, Hosoya. "The Tripartite Pact, 1939–1940." In James William Morley, ed. *Deterrent Diplomacy: Japan, Germany, and the USSR, 1935–1940.* New York: Columbia University Press, 1976, pp. 181–257.

Fletcher, William Miles III. *The Search for a New Order: Intellectuals and Fascism in Prewar Japan.* Chapel Hill: University of North Carolina Press, 1982.

Hotta, Eri. *Japan 1941: Countdown to Infamy.* New York: Knopf, 2013.

Ikuhiko, Hata. "The Army's Move into Northern Indochina." In James William Morley, ed. *The Fateful Choice: Japan's Advance into Southeast Asia, 1939–1941.* New York: Columbia University Press, 1980, pp. 155–207.

Iriye, Akira. *Power and Culture: The Japanese-American War, 1941–1945.* Cambridge, MA: Harvard University Press, 1981.

Katsumi, Usui. "The Politics of War, 1937–1941." In James William Morley, ed. *The China Quagmire: Japan's Expansion on the Asian Continent, 1933–1941.* New York: Columbia University Press, 1983, pp. 287–435.

Mitter, Rana. *Forgotten Ally: China's World War II, 1937–1945.* Boston: Houghton Mifflin, 2013.

Shillony, Ben-Ami. *Politics and Culture in Wartime Japan.* Oxford: Oxford University Press, 1981.

Shinjirō, Nagaoka. "The Drive into Southern Indochina and Thailand." In James William Morley, ed., *The Fateful Choice: Japan's Advance into Southeast Asia, 1939–1941.* New York: Columbia University Press, 1980, pp. 209–40.

Shinjirō, Nagaoka. "Economic Demands on the Dutch East Indies." In James William Morley, ed. *The Fateful Choice: Japan's Advance into Southeast Asia, 1939–1941.* New York: Columbia University Press, 1980, pp. 125–53.

Sun, Youli. *China and the Origins of the Pacific War, 1931–1941.* New York: St. Martin's, 1993, chap. 7.

ACKNOWLEDGMENTS

I began work on this game more than eleven years ago, and during that time it has been reviewed by numerous academics and play-tested in a great many classrooms. There is no way I can thank everyone who has helped me along the way, but I want to express particular gratitude to Michael Barnhart of SUNY-Stony Brook, Dennis Frost of Kalamazoo College, Brian Hoffert of North Central College, Nicolas Proctor of Simpson College, Mathew Thompson of Sophia University, and Paul Wright of Cabrini College. I have also had the great fortune of being able to use the game in several of my courses on East Asian history, and my students have had a massive influence how it has developed, particularly Caleb Boyer, Reid Courtney, Jackie Dambrosio, Jared Deeds, Samantha Eron, Logan Finley, Katie Fossaceca, Devin Hill, Zach Humrichouser, McKenzie Jones, Jakson Kennedy, Brennan Kunkel, Brian Le, Sophia Leddy, Catie Lewis, Tyler MacQueen, Kristen Marshall, Doug Martonik, Josh Mason, James Metzger, C. J. Murnane, Rick Platt, Sean Quigley, David Reeves, Matt Rhyand, Devin Scott, Kasey Siciliano, Kitty Sorah, Colin Suffecool, Nick Thielman, Lucas Trott, Abby Wilhelm, Tucker Wilkinson, and Rebecca Young. The staff of the Reacting to the Past Consortium, especially Mark Carnes, Jennifer Worth, and Madalena Provo, have been constant sources of support, and I am highly appreciative for the study leave provided by my employer, Ashland University, to complete the manuscript. Thanks to Justin Cahill, Angie Merila, and Candace Levy of W. W. Norton for making the publication process reasonably stress free. Finally, I am eternally grateful to my wife, Monica, and my daughter, Constanze, who make all of my efforts worthwhile.

NOTES

1. Fukuzawa quoted in Carmen Blacker, *The Japanese Enlightenment: A Study of the Writings of Fukuzawa Yukichi* (London: Cambridge University Press, 1964), p. 31.

2. Ibid., pp. 31–32.

3. Motoda quoted in David S. Nivison and Arthur F. Wright, eds., *Confucianism in Action* (Stanford, CA: Stanford University Press, 1959), p. 327. *Filial piety* means reverence for one's parents, a central tenet of East Asian thought going back at least as far as Confucius.

4. Blacker, *The Japanese Enlightenment*, p. 49.

5. Inazō Nitobe, *Bushido: Samurai Ethics and the Soul of Japan* (Mineola, NY: Dover Publications, 2004), p. 45.

6. Yamamoto Tsunetomo, *Hagakure: The Book of the Samurai* (Tokyo: Kodansha International, 1992), p. 23.

7. Ibid., p. 26.

8. Richard Storry, *The Double Patriots: A Study of Japanese Nationalism* (London: Chatto & Windus, 1957), pp. 3–4.

9. In the short term, aid to China from the Soviet Union was more significant. Stalin's government sought concessions from the Chinese Nationalists and believed that aid in the fight against Japan was the best way to secure them. Between 1937 and 1939 the Soviets extended some $250 million in loans to Jiang's regime and sent roughly 900 aircraft as well.

10. Storry, *The Double Patriots*, p. 4.

11. This is a slight counterfactual. In July 1940 Admiral Yoshida Zengo held the post of navy minister, but Yoshida stepped down in early September after suffering what appears to have been a nervous breakdown.

12. Prince Fushimi Hiroyasu is an anomaly—as an active-duty admiral he is a member of the Navy faction (indeed, he is navy chief of staff), but as the emperor's cousin, he is also a member of the Imperial Court.

13. In games with only twelve players Nagano begins as navy chief of staff.

CREDITS

Amur Society: "An Anniversary Statement by the Amur Society" from *Sources of Japanese Tradition, 2nd Ed., Vol. 2, Abridged, Part 2*, by Wm. Theodore de Bary, Carol Gluck, and Arthur E. Tiedemann. Copyright © 2006 Columbia University Press. Reprinted with permission of the publisher.

Robert King Hall (ed.): *Kokutai No Hongi: Cardinal Principles of the National Entity of Japan*, translated by John Owen Gauntlett, and edited with an introduction by Robert King Hall, Cambridge, Mass.: Harvard University Press, Copyright © 1949 by the President and Fellows of Harvard College, Copyright © renewed 1977 by Robert King Hall.

Kita Ikki: "An Outline Plan for the Reorganization of Japan" from *Sources of Japanese Tradition, 2nd Ed., Vol. 2, Abridged, Part 2*, by Wm. Theodore de Bary, Carol Gluck, and Arthur E. Tiedemann. Copyright © 2006 Columbia University Press. Reprinted with permission of the publisher.

Japanese Army Ministry: "On the Basic Meaning of National Defense and Its Intensification" from *Sources of Japanese Tradition, 2nd Ed., Vol. 2, Abridged, Part 2*, by Wm. Theodore de Bary, Carol Gluck, and Arthur E. Tiedemann. Copyright © 2006 Columbia University Press. Reprinted with permission of the publisher.

Miyazaki Masayoshi: "Toa Renmei Ron (On the East Asian League)," translated by Michael A. Schneider. From *Pan-Asianism: A Documentary History, Volume 2*, edited by Sven Saaler and Christopher W. A. Szpilman. Copyright © 2011 by Rowman & Littlefield Publishers, Inc. Reproduced with permission of the Licensor through PLSclear.

Takeda Nobushige: "Opinions in Ninety-Nine Articles," from *Ideals of the Samurai: Writings of Japanese Warriors* (Ohara, 1982). Translated by William Scott Wilson. Republished by permission of William Scott Wilson.

Asakura Norikage: "The Recorded Words of Asakura Soteki," from *Ideals of the Samurai: Writings of Japanese Warriors* (Ohara, 1982). Translated by William Scott Wilson. Republished by permission of William Scott Wilson.

Nagai Ryūtarō: "Holy War for the Reconstruction of Asia," translated by Roger H. Brown. From *Pan-Asianism: A Documentary History, Volume 2*, edited by Sven Saaler and Christopher W. A. Szpilman. Copyright © 2011 by Rowman & Littlefield Publishers, Inc. Reproduced with permission of the Licensor through PLSclear.

Ryū Shintarō: "Japan's Economic Reorganization" from *Sources of Japanese Tradition, 2nd Ed., Vol. 2, Abridged, Part 2*, by Wm. Theodore de Bary, Carol Gluck, and Arthur E. Tiedemann. Copyright © 2006 Columbia University Press. Reprinted with permission of the publisher.

Asakura Toshikage: "The Seventeen Articles of Asakura Toshikage," from *Ideals of the Samurai: Writings of Japanese Warriors* (Ohara, 1982). Translated by William Scott Wilson. Republished by permission of William Scott Wilson.

CPSIA information can be obtained
at www.ICGtesting.com
Printed in the USA
LVHW020053070722
722852LV00005B/112